POTTER HEIGHAM

THE OFFICIAL **NATIONAL PARK GUIDE**

THE BROADS

Text by Clive Tully · Photographs by Richard Denyer

SERIES EDITOR ROLY SMITH

PEVENSEY GUIDES

The original Broads Authority was
established in 1978. Following the
Broads Act 1988, the Broads took on
new status equivalent to a national park
in 1989. From April 2002, the
organisation has agreed to take the
new name of the Broads National Park.

The Pevensey Press is an imprint of
David & Charles

First published in the UK in 2002

Map artwork by Ethan Danielson
based on material supplied by the
Broads Authority

ISBN 1 898630 20 8 (paperback)

Edited by Sue Viccars
Book design by Les Dominey Design
Company, Exeter
and Printed in China by
CT Printing Ltd.
for David & Charles
Brunel House Newton Abbot Devon

Contents

Front cover: (top) Halvergate Marshes; (below) Before the start: The Yare Navigation Race at Coldham Hall; (front flap) The North Sea at Waxham
Back cover: Salt marshes at Thornham, north Norfolk coast

Page 1: Potter Heigham village sign
Pages 2–3: West Somerton dyke
Left: Horsey windpump

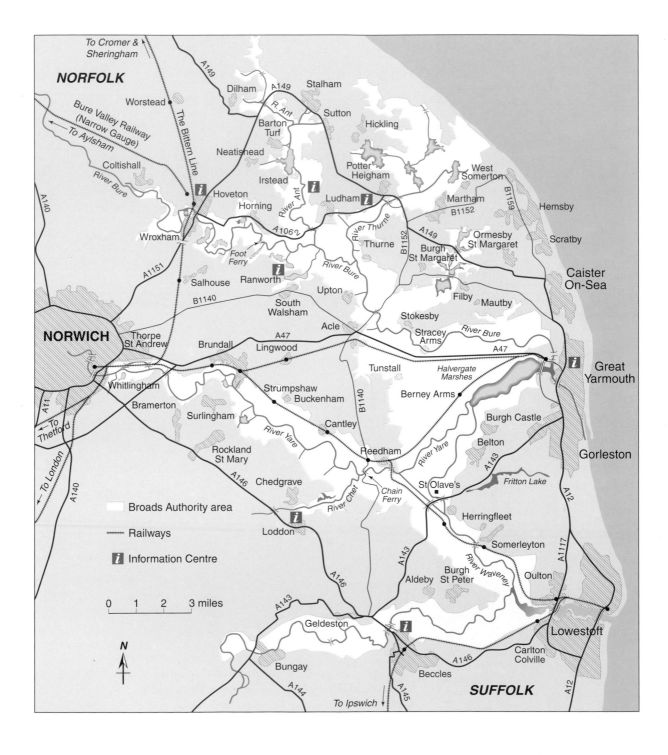

Foreword

by Martin Fitton, Chief Executive, Association of National Park Authorities

The Norfolk and Suffolk Broads is one of our finest landscapes, with its mixture of water, wetlands and wildlife all presented in this guide for your enjoyment. It is one of a number of areas we specially protect as National Parks and they form the highest rank of protected areas, established by Parliament in 1949.

Our National Parks are doubly special. Unlike many in the world, they are landscapes created and largely maintained, by humans, mainly through farming. They are 'living landscapes', where change occurs through development in the small towns and villages and through changes in agricultural and forestry practices. So when you visit the Broads, remember that you are not simply looking at a beautiful landscape. You are seeing a place where people have lived and worked over many centuries.

Change has not always worked to the advantage of the National Parks. For example, agricultural intensification and development has had a major effect on water quality, which has required much effort by the Broads National Park to rectify. Part of this problem was created by changes in farming policy. This obliged farmers to produce more in order to maintain an adequate standard of living. These policies are now changing, however, and the role farmers play in maintaining these beautiful landscapes is now recognised and funding is being provided to help them to do this.

National Parks are now cared for by independent planning authorities which hold land, provide grants to farmers and others; provide rangers, information, car parks and toilets; clear footpaths and litter, plant trees and partner many other agencies in pursuit of the purposes for which they exist. They are there to conserve natural beauty, wildlife and cultural heritage and to promote the Parks' enjoyment by the public while fostering the social and economic well-being of their residents.

As a visitor, you can help sustain this wonderful landscape. Simply by being there, you are helping the local economy. You can help even more if you make a special effort to find and purchase local goods and services. Celebrate the fact that this is an environment producing good quality local food. This will mean that you become a more 'sustainable' tourist - a jargon word that expresses the challenging thought that we can look after the environment while enjoying the beauty of the countryside.

It is a pleasure to welcome you to the Broads, and I trust that this guide will add to your enjoyment.

Introducing The Broads

It's hard to imagine as you gaze at a tranquil Broads setting that what you're looking at isn't in fact the most perfect natural landscape. Beautiful lakes fringed with reeds gently swaying in the breeze, an abundance of plants and birdlife, deciduous woodland – how could it be anything else?

But as you move along the waterways which join these lakes, or broads, you start to pick up odd clues that indicate a different story. Here and there the waterways have an unnaturally straight look to them, and you might make a connection with the numerous 'windmills' which dot the countryside. They're actually drainage mills, a type of windpump, and they do have a lot to do with the shaping of the landscape.

In fact, the Broads is one of the best examples in the country of an industrial landscape, softened by

Above: All Saints, Billockby
Opposite: Eric Edwards cutting reed at How Hill on the River Ant
Below: Nutmeg environmental puppet show, Beccles

centuries of drainage, the development of arable farming and, lately, interest in keeping the grazing marshes. While the assumption up until comparatively recently was that they were natural lakes, the broads themselves are actually the result of peat-digging in the Middle Ages, carried out on a scale which could best be described as industrial.

It went on for around 500 years, roughly from the reign of Alfred the Great to that of Henry V. The peat came from pretty boggy ground anyway, which had the tendency to flood as the peat was dug out. By the end of the peat-digging period, it was becoming harder and harder to extract, till it reached the point where the diggings were abandoned one by one. Their fate was sealed when the sea level rose, gradually turning them into the peaceful expanses of water we know today. The surrounding fens are largely the result of constant reed-cutting; Norfolk reed has been used for thatching for hundreds of years, and it's still the best natural thatching material you can get. Left to its own devices, the fenland surrounding the Broads would gradually turn into woodland over a period of about twenty-five years.

A UNIQUE LANDSCAPE

When you stack it up against the big upland National Parks of England and Wales, there's no comparison – the Broads is unique. Here there are no lofty peaks, no waterfalls tumbling down craggy rock faces, no wild and mysterious moorlands. Totally different from the spectacular mountain scenery of the Lake District and Snowdonia, or the wild windswept moors of Dartmoor or the North York Moors, there's no part of the Broads very far removed from 'civilisation'. Even so, there are many parts of the area which engender the most wonderful feelings of isolation.

The late Norfolk naturalist Ted Ellis described the Broads as 'a breathing space for the cure of souls', and certainly many would ascribe a spiritual quality

to their experiences there. It is still possible, even at the height of summer when holiday traffic at its busiest, to get away from it all. But come here at either end of the season, or even in the winter, and you will understand how a glistening frost and pastel sky can grip the imagination.

Small wonder that so many artists have been inspired by the Broads. Art galleries in Norwich and elsewhere will almost certainly number Broads landscapes among their exhibits, and historically we have famous artists such as Crome, Cotman, Bright and Stannard, some of the best-known members of the famous Norwich School of artists. Many of their works were scenes from the Broads, and can be viewed in Norwich Castle Museum.

Photographers have found inspiration here, too. G. Christopher Davies was described in his obituary as 'the man who found the Broads'. Apart from starting off the trend in Broads guidebooks (his *Handbook to the Rivers and Broads of Norfolk and Suffolk* went to no fewer than fifty editions), he was the first of the great Broads photographers, although many would regard the Cuban-born American P.H. Emerson as the definitive one. He immersed himself in his subjects, and his atmospheric and evocative photographs captured the mood and essence of the Broads in a characteristic style which has been imitated by other photographers many times since.

Some of the broads have a marvellously intimate quality, wooded around the edges and fringed with swaying reeds, while elsewhere, particularly the marshy areas closer to the coast, there is a wide open feel, with isolated windpumps and grazing cows adding to the distinctive character. Here you can be

Below: St Benet's Abbey, River Bure

Above: Malthouse Broad, Ranworth

walking along a field edge when suddenly, a sail appears, apparently creeping across the fields. Some are isolated pools, others much larger. Linked together by the Rivers Yare, Waveney, Bure, Thurne, Chet and Ant, along with artificial cuttings called dykes, the Broads waterways meander across Norfolk and Suffolk, until they disgorge into the mudflats of Breydon Water, and then into the North Sea at Great Yarmouth.

In the days when the rivers were an important part of the transportation network, the workhorse cargo boats were sailing wherries. Unlike the barges used on other waterways, the wherries were clinker-built, usually put together on the river banks without any plans, and with nothing more than the builder's seasoned eye to ensure the hull was true. The wherries were purpose-built for their working environment, and often very fast. They'd have a large black gaff mainsail on a mast, hinged and counterbalanced with a huge weight in order to make passing under the numerous bridges spanning the rivers possible. Typical cargoes were coal, timber, bricks, grain and beet. Changes in the types of cargo carried and the development of roads and railways spelled the end of the line for the sailing wherries. The last was built in 1912, and they continued working the rivers up until World War II, although by then most of those remaining had engines.

THE GROWTH OF TOURISM

While Great Yarmouth's popularity as a seaside resort goes all the way back to the middle of the eighteenth century, when the first bath house was built, it wasn't until around 100 years later that mass tourism to the area really took off. The newly built railways brought families escaping the industrial

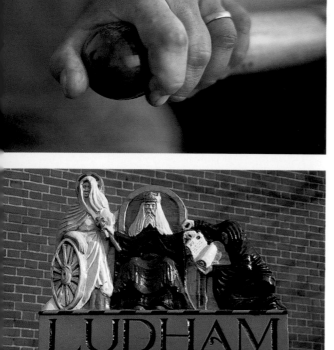

Top: Hand on the tiller
Above: Ludham village sign
Opposite: Wind farm, Winterton

Midlands and North, and while the majority stuck to the beaches, public gardens and inns of Yarmouth and Lowestoft, some discovered the 'other world' delights of the Broads.

Even so, recreation for the local folk goes a lot further back. Water frolics, which involved racing in boats, various entertainments, and doubtless much drinking, can be traced back to the late sixteenth century. In 1821 the Thorpe Frolic on the River Yare just outside Norwich is said to have attracted 20,000 people – a sizeable chunk of the city's population.

In general, the Broads has always regarded tourism as a more refined pursuit. The business of hiring boats for cruising started out in the late 1870s. It wasn't just small boats that were made available for hire, either; some wherry operators scrubbed out the holds of their boats, fitted partitions and kitted out the resulting cabins with hammocks so that the boats could be let out during the summer for pleasure cruising. The idea clearly caught on; it led first to trading wherries being permanently converted to pleasure use and, later, to purpose-made pleasure wherries being built.

In late Victorian and early Edwardian times tastes became somewhat more sophisticated. So the pleasure wherry evolved into the more up-market wherry yacht – the same wherry rig to propel it, but a sleeker hull – and with an afterdeck, the perfect place to enjoy a drink without interfering with the activities of those actually engaged in the business of sailing the craft. For many years the *Albion* was the only trading wherry left afloat on the Broads, although after a long period of restoration she has been joined by the *Maud*. There are also six surviving pleasure wherries and wherry yachts.

But not everybody wanted, or could afford, to hire a craft as big as a wherry. John Loynes pioneered the hiring of small sailing boats at the end of the nineteenth century, and in 1908 Blakes, a company which exists to this day, set themselves up to act as agents for boat hire companies. The next revolution came in the twenties and thirties, when motor cruisers appeared on the scene. Now anybody could get afloat on the Broads - you didn't need the same level of skill to operate a motor boat.

It wasn't until after World War II that cruising really took off as a mass-market pursuit – as paid holidays became available to everyone as a right, and more people took to the roads as well as railways in search of recreational pursuits. In the 1960s boat production was revolutionised, made faster and cheaper with the introduction of glass-fibre mouldings, thus doing away with the labour-intensive traditional methods of boat-building.

In all, something like 125 miles (200km) of Broads waterways are navigable by boats, the largest system of inland waterways in Britain without locks. In recent years, however, cruising holidays on the Broads have declined as recreational tastes have changed. Boat operators have been encouraged to develop hulls which produce less wash, which over the years has contributed to river-

bank erosion, and much investment in modern boats is being made in cruising holidays on the Broads to enable them to survive into the new century.

But as hire cruising has scaled back, general leisure boating on the Broads has increased dramatically, and it's not hard to see why. It is a safe place for the less experienced and those wishing to learn, but can also provide the means to test the more advanced sailors, such as the frequent necessity to manoeuvre in tight spaces, often quickly.

A POSITIVE FUTURE

All the National Parks have to make sure that the economic considerations of what is, after all, a working landscape, and the interests of tourism and recreation, don't outweigh those of conservation. After all, it's the beautiful landscape we come to admire. In the Broads, this juggling act is a good deal more tricky, since the fragile ecosystems are all dependent on the quality of the water which sadly, over the years, has suffered. To its credit, the Broads Authority has made significant steps in recent years to try to improve the water quality of many of the broads.

Above: How Hill environmental education centre
Opposite: Horsey windpump

While motor boats are a factor in erosion of the river banks, other factors have also had a damaging effect on the Broads environment. Phosphates from sewage treatment works, combined with nitrates from agricultural fertilisers, has encouraged the growth of algae. This effectively choked the growth of other aquatic plantlife, so breaking the food chain for fish, insects and wildfowl.

Agricultural drainage too has played its part. In the early 1980s much of the grazing marshland of the Broads was turned over from uneconomic cattle pasture to arable farming, which at the time attracted huge grants as part of the European Union's Common Agricultural Policy. The dykes which criss-cross the marshes support a wide variety of wildlife, some species of which came close to extinction in the face of this onslaught. The risk was that as the wetlands were drained they became arable 'prairies', incapable of providing a hospitable wildlife habitat. If you get to hear the eerie booming call of the male bittern, a bird akin to a heron, when you visit the Broads, you'll be privileged indeed. Numbers have declined to around twenty. Likewise, the swallowtail butterfly is another endangered species. In both cases, the reduction in numbers is down to changes in their habitats.

The Broads Authority rose to the challenge and came up with a policy of positive conservation management, in contrast to the previous compensation payments. The area is now managed as traditional grazing marshland, and the scheme was so successful it was adopted as the national model for Environmentally Sensitive Areas (ESAs).

Above: Norwich bypass: A47 viaduct over the River Yare
Opposite: Whitebeam, near Chedgrave

When the first prime areas of the British landscape were being considered for National Park designation back in the late 1940s, the Broads was among those in the running. Amazingly it failed to make the final list, and another forty years passed before its unique value was recognised, during which time the area had come under considerable environmental pressure.

The Broads took on a status equivalent to a National Park in 1989, but while they're called National Parks in Britain, they're neither parks in the accepted sense of the word, nor does the title 'national' mean that they're owned by the nation. In the United States, for example, the meaning is rather more clear-cut. In the crowded little island of Britain, we have to accept that our treasured landscapes are a patchwork in terms of ownership and usage, and that people live and work in them as well. National Park Authorities have to balance what at times can be conflicting interests: those of conservation, tourism, commerce and planning.

But the Broads have an extra dimension, the fact that part of the area which falls within the Broads Authority remit is water rather than land. Those 125 miles (200km) of navigable waterways are utilised by thousands of pleasure craft. Water is taken out via boreholes from the surrounding area, and waste water finds its way back into the system through water treatment plants. Then there's the chemical-rich run-off from surrounding agricultural land, not to mention the increasing risk of flooding as the sea level gradually creeps higher.

All these factors combine to present the Broads with a unique set of problems, which are being met with unique solutions as the Broads Authority

institutes a number of long-term plans to improve the water quality. These include mud pumping, and the creation of conditions in which water fleas, whose appetite for algae is prodigious, can flourish. Also sewage-treatment plants now have the means to strip phosphates out of the water. Hopefully these measures and others will keep Britain's most prized wetland safe and beautiful for future generations to enjoy.

One of the Broads Authority's great early successes was at Cockshoot Broad, near Horning. It was dammed off from the river and about 3ft (1m) of mud was pumped out. Within three months, seeds which had lain dormant at the bottom of the broad for decades started to shoot, and the water became clear again. Suction dredging has been used successfully at a number of locations, and recently the Broads Authority has concluded an ambitious five-year project at Barton Broad, the second largest of the broads, restoring the water quality and aquatic wildlife.

It would be wrong to suppose that everything that makes the Broads what they are boils down to the natural environment. The buildings play their part too, from isolated windpumps on the marshes, and the rustic chalets and boat sheds that line the river banks at places like Horning, to the churches, with Ranworth undoubtedly the finest. And yes, even the bustling boating centres and boatyards which make so many cruising holidays possible, have their place, contributing towards the look and feel of a unique area.

Right: Toad Hole cottage, How Hill estate
Opposite: The wherry Norada *negotiating Mutford Lock, Oulton Broad, near Lowestoft*

I The making of The Broads

S itting in the viewing gallery at the Broads Wildlife Centre, your binoculars trained on a coot as it moves across the serene, reed-fringed waters of Ranworth Inner Broad, it's almost impossible to imagine that the scene before your eyes could be anything other than Nature at her very best. But the truth is that this placid lake, along with the other broads, was not hewn out of the ground by natural forces. It was dug out, bit by bit, in a medieval quest for fuel.

Unlike the other National Parks, the Broads landscape hasn't been defined by ancient rocks going through tortuous upheaval millions of years ago, even though geological movements have influenced the rise and fall in the sea level which overlooked their creation. It's all a lot younger than that. In fact, at the time of the Romans, a mere 2,000 years ago, most of the area now occupied by the Broads lay under water. The rivers which now form the backbone of the area ran into a huge estuary known as *Gariensis*, which probably had several outlets on the coast between Waxham and Lowestoft, but with its principal outflow bounded at the coast on its north shore by Caister-on-Sea, and Burgh Castle to the south.

Caister was an important port conveniently placed for trade with Europe, but in fact it was as much a stopping-off point for ships rather than a final destination, since it was at the time built on an otherwise uninhabited island. In the third century, when Roman Britain was being threatened by incursions from raiders, *Gariannonum*, the Saxon shore fort at Burgh Castle, was built. Its massive walls of local flint and Roman red tile enclosed an area of 6 acres (2.5ha), looking west across Breydon Water. But, as elsewhere, the Romans' influence in Britain was waning. As a result of there being insufficient troops, the line of Saxon shore forts which stretched from Brancaster on the north Norfolk coast, to Portchester in Hampshire, was manned by mercenaries. Burgh Castle, for example, was garrisoned by a unit of Stablesian cavalry, originally from what is now Yugoslavia. Where Angles and Saxons had already

Above: Swan and cygnets, How Hill estate
Right: Burgh Castle and Berney Arms windpump

settled, the Romans used grants of land and housing to entice them into helping defend against further outside incursions, but the die was already cast. Many of them agreed, simply biding their time until they were in a position to take control themselves.

Up till then, the region's capital was *Venta Icenorum*, just south of what was to become Norwich, but on the whole the area was still sparsely populated. The 'uplands' around the heads of the river valleys of the Yare, Bure, Ant and Waveney were a mixture of wood and heathland, and it was only by the time that the Danes arrived in the eighth century that things picked up. The population increased, as did the amount of wood cutting for fuel.

During this time the sea level dropped sufficiently to allow the development of mudflats and low-lying marshes, and gradually settlers moved in to make use of it. At the same time, a spit of sand and shingle was building up in the middle of that great river mouth which in time

Above: The Red Mill, Reedham Ferry
Left: North Walsham & Dilham Canal

would become Great Yarmouth. In just a few hundred years, that once-mighty estuary dwindled to the tidal lake which is Breydon Water, inland from Yarmouth.

Some 1,650ft (500m) below the surface lie the oldest rock strata of the Broads, the Precambrian layer known as the Anglo-Brabant Massif. That, and the layers of Silurian, Permian and Carboniferous rocks above it, have very little influence on the shaping of the area. But on top of that lies a 1,300ft- (400m) deep layer of chalk. The water which supplies the Broads rivers comes from aquifers in this chalk, and in modern times, the groundwater which lies in this porous rock has been extracted from boreholes to provide drinking water. In places the chalk occurs as outcrops, which over the years have been quarried for building materials, but elsewhere it is covered with a layer of chalky boulder clay, deposited during successive Ice Ages. The river valleys at the time were steeper, and the rivers faster flowing, while the land was covered with thick vegetation and forest. But as the sea level rose tidal influences moved further upstream, and the vegetation alongside the rivers was overwhelmed by the tide-deposited sediment. That in turn became a rich layer of peat.

In a *History of Norfolk* written in 1854, the origins of the Broads were described thus: 'Most of the rivers rise in marshy land, and running through a comparatively level country, the fall is consequently small, and their current slow; so that they contribute to keep the adjacent grounds in a swampy state,

Above: Tonnage bridge, River Ant

and fill the atmosphere with noxious vapours. When swelled by land floods, their estuaries being for the most part choked with silt driven up by the violence of the tide, they often overflow the low lands, and in their course form numerous small shallow lakes, or pools, provincially termed "broads, or medes".'

Indeed, even up until around forty years ago, it was supposed that the shallow lakes which are the Broads were formed simply as a result of patches of that great estuary being left behind when the sea level fell. Despite all the documentary evidence of turf-cutting, there were still plenty of people who refused to believe that the broads could be anything other than natural lakes. So how was it that their history was so dramatically and decisively rewritten?

A STARTLING DISCOVERY

Back in the 1950s, botanist Dr Joyce Lambert was studying peat deposits for their plantlife, and making a series of closely spaced borings around Surlingham Broad. What she found was somewhat unexpected, so she checked her results elsewhere. After some 2,000 borings conducted in different broads, she came to the conclusion that the lakes were not natural at all. Although smoothed off by accumulations of mud, what lay beneath were peat bottoms around 8–12ft (2.5–3.5m) down – unnaturally level – and with stepped or vertical sides.

Some broads also featured 'islands' and peninsulas of uncut peat, several of which were crossed with thin parallel ridges, or balks, which were shown from medieval estate maps to be lines of demarcation, or strip-parcelling. Had the broads been the leftovers of a much larger watercourse, it would be logical to assume that the lakes would have been left behind with the Broadland rivers running straight through them. But they are all to the sides of the main rivers; the close proximity to water lends weight to the assumption that the peat was cut not just for domestic consumption, but for distribution further afield by boat. The pits themselves were separated from the rivers by banks or 'ronds' of impervious clay, so there was little lateral seepage of water.

The final part of the jigsaw, the connection of the broads to the river system, undoubtedly took place over subsequent generations, with channels dug by wildfowlers and fishermen out to improve their lot, and thatchers wanting easier access to the rich abundance of reeds which grew along the fringes of the broads. Dr Lambert's findings were published in 1960 in a book entitled *The Making of the Broads*, co-authored with J. N. Jennings, C. T. Smith, Charles Green and J. N. Hutchinson.

THE PEAT INDUSTRY

At the time, the findings were greeted with a good deal of incredulity. How could such vast expanses of water have been created by hand digging? Smith had calculated that some 900 million cubic feet of peat must have been removed. Apart from the sheer scale of the operation needed to extract such massive quantities, there was also the intriguing question of where it all went. Surely the demand could not have been that great?

The problem was that by the eleventh century there was little in the way of fuel to satisfy the needs of a rapidly growing population. At the time, Norfolk and Suffolk were the most densely populated counties in the country. After the Norman Conquest, Norwich expanded quickly, and its cathedral and surrounding monasteries needed fuel for their fires to ward off the bitter chill of the winter winds which blew in off the North Sea. Although the Domesday Book doesn't actually refer to it in great depth, we do know that peat-diggings were becoming the main sources of fuel since most of the woodlands had already been cleared for use as fuel and to permit agriculture.

Smith based his calculations on the premise that around 14,000 families lived in the Broads area during medieval times, and that each would need around 8,000 turves a year to satisfy their own requirements. On the basis of

FOR PEAT'S SAKE

Peat is a spongy, organic, fibrous material formed by the incomplete decomposition of plants in poorly drained areas. It's the first stage towards the formation of coal, but for that to happen the peat needs to be covered by sediments laid down by rising seas, and for the whole lot to be subjected to considerable pressure for several million years. The peat which exists now began to be formed after the glaciers retreated from the last Ice Age around 10,000 years ago. As plants died and fell into the boggy waters, they did not rot away completely, but decomposed partially due to the level of acidity and lack of oxygen. This vegetation then turned into peat, some of it brown and spongy, elsewhere, black and compacted, dependent on the degree of decomposition.

Over the centuries peat has been used as fuel in areas where coal or wood was in short supply, hence the extensive diggings in Norfolk after the forests were cut down. In its natural state, peat contains up to 95 per cent water, so after it was cut into blocks it would then be laid out to dry. Its calorific value is around two thirds that of coal, consequently larger volumes are needed to produce the same amount of heat. If stacked up, the amount needed to heat a house for the winter would probably be as big as the house itself.

Left: Village signs – Halvergate, West Somerton and Potter Heigham

all the broads being dug for peat to a depth of around 6–10ft (2–3m), he surmised that the peat could have lasted for around 350 years.

Apart from anything else, there is a wealth of documentary evidence to show that peat was being burnt in large quantities by medieval times. Norwich Cathedral Priory records for the thirteenth and fourteenth centuries show that 400,000 turves of peat were being burned every year. A peat-digging was called a turbary, a word which crops up in a number of documents of the time, some of them relating to various manors throughout the Broads, and the telling part is the fact that they are all places where broads exist now. Those parishes recorded as having turbaries but no broads of their own probably had the rights to cut the turf elsewhere. So not only was peat being dug for local consumption, there was a thriving trade in it as well.

At South Walsham, for example, records for the second half of the thirteenth century show an average sale of 200,000 turves a year. That was far more than what the local inhabitants needed for their own use, and it produced an income of £7 a year for the Manor. In fact the income from the sale of turves was far greater than that from livestock, and was exceeded by the income from the sale of grain in years when the harvest was good. In both Norwich and Great Yarmouth, murage – a tax on goods to pay for maintenance on the walls – was levied on the carriage of peat.

It was a major industry, with every settlement digging its own peat for local consumption and trade. Huge quantities were sold to Norwich, and the salt pans along the mudflats on the lower reaches of the Broads rivers would have needed a good supply as well – boiling brine would speed up the evaporation process which produced salt. With harsh winters to contend with, it was easier to slaughter livestock rather than keep animals alive until needed. But preserving meat meant a big demand for salt, and therefore for peat. In places such as Heigham Sound, where the underlying clay was being dug out for bricks and pottery (recalled in the name Potter Heigham), peat would undoubtedly have been used to fire the kilns.

Although the major part of the Broads peat-digging occurred in the Middle Ages, it is quite likely it was going on as long ago as the ninth century on a smaller scale. This part of East Anglia was invaded by Danes, as evidenced by the number of place names ending in 'by', such as Rollesby and Filby. And although it is only speculation, the Danes were masters at cutting peat in their native country, where evidence of the practice goes back as far as 500BC.

Initially it would have been relatively easy to cut the peat using the crude tools of the time. But as the pits became deeper they tended to fill with water, a problem which became exacerbated as the sea level began to rise once more. Even before this, some means of keeping the peat workings free from water would have been necessary. With the diggings going down to almost 10ft (3m), they would still have been below the water table, and there would have been a tendency to flood anyway. Although no evidence has been found, it is possible that they would have used some means to bale out the water, perhaps like the ladle-and-gantry system used until relatively recently in the peat-diggings in the Somerset Levels. Here, a bucket scoop suspended on a rope from a supporting frame provided a basic means for shifting the water which collected in the diggings through natural seepage.

Not all the broads had the same propensity to flooding. Those lying in side valleys, separated from the main rivers by thick layers of clay, were less prone,

Pages 26–7: Medieval bridge, Potter Heigham, River Thurne
Below: Flint wall, St Benet's Abbey

and they could also be drained by diverting streams away from the diggings.

The inundation which gradually took over the peat-diggings wouldn't have happened all at once. Periodic sea surges would have provoked major flooding over the years. The thirteenth century saw the most, ending several centuries of surges resulting from a warmer climate. One in 1287 proved particularly catastrophic, and undoubtedly would have had a severe impact on the industry. John of Oxenedes, one of the monks at St Benet's Abbey, described the widespread flooding which occurred when the sea broke into the Broads area; and it is quite likely that this particular flood marked the beginning of the end for the peat industry. The early part of the fourteenth century also saw increasing amounts of rainfall as the weather deteriorated generally. River levels and the general water table rose, and that combined with the general rise in sea level which was under way.

When Joyce Lambert and her colleagues were piecing all this together they had to find concrete evidence that the sea level was indeed lower in medieval times than it is now. As she and Jennings stated in *The Making of the Broads*: 'The sheer size and depth of the basins point either to more favourable conditions for the deep digging of peat at some time in the past than at the present day in East Norfolk valleys, or else to the unlikely engineering in early historical times of effective methods for preventing continual flooding while the pits were being worked.'

They examined various artifacts around Great Yarmouth, including the buried remains of two ships and the foundations of the town wall. The hypothesis was clinched when they looked at a mid-seventeenth-century well. The bottom of the well was constructed at the point where the foot or so of freshwater floated on top of the saline groundwater. This paved base now lies more than 2ft (0.6m) below the level of saltwater, which suggests that the level of the sea has risen in relation to the land. In medieval times, the land could have been 10–13ft (3–4m) higher in relation to the sea than it is now.

Excavations for the foundations of Great Yarmouth's power station on South Denes in the 1950s added weight to the findings. Deposits of pottery

Above, left to right: St Helen's, Ranworth; Green Man, St Nicholas, Potter Heigham; All Saints, Chedgrave; St Mary's, Haddiscoe

BRAND NEW BROADS

The original broads may have come about through necessity, but at Whitlingham, just south east of Norwich on the River Yare, brand new broads – the first in centuries – are taking shape in the name of recreation. Whitlingham Little Broad, already complete, hosts a number of non-powered watersports, including sailing, windsurfing, and kayaking. Whitlingham Great Broad, due to be finished in 2006, is going to be quite a sight at 1,750yd (1,600m) long. While it too will be host to all manner of watersports, it, and the surrounding 280-acre (113-hectare) Whitlingham Country Park, is designed to attract wildlife as well as well as those seeking a modern breathing space.

fragments dating from the thirteenth century were found in a layer of sand above a layer of barnacle-covered stones and pottery some 13–17ft (4–5m) below the current sea level.

So as the sea level began to rise the industry continued, with nets on poles taking the place of spades, but instead of being cut in solid chunks the peat was dredged out of the pits in a soggy mass, then poured into moulds and dried out. But eventually even that became impracticable. Of all the documentary evidence that exists, none seems to point to the formation of the broads before the fourteenth century, and certainly they don't appear on any maps until the fifteenth and sixteenth centuries.

The lands of the Great Hospital of Norwich at Wroxham and Salhouse were described in documents from the fourteenth century as containing turbary, whilst a century later they were described as 'water and marsh'. It may be, given the change in the means to extract peat, that what was being described was essentially the same, but certainly they indicate that change was under way. And elsewhere, where turbaries were once mentioned, fisheries had taken over. By the sixteenth century, when detailed surveys were relatively abundant, turf-cutting doesn't feature at all. Clearly, as the flooded peat-diggings became uneconomic to work for peat, their role transformed.

Looking back at historical references, the name 'broad' doesn't even crop up until comparatively recently. Sir Thomas Browne mentions 'broads' or 'broadwaters' in his *Natural History of Norfolk*, published around 1670. Not that he gave any clues as to their origin. Prior to that, the term 'broding' crops up in estate maps.

As Dr Lambert and her colleagues considered these various pieces of evidence, they came to the conclusion that the only possible explanation for the broads was that they were man-made. Despite the layer of mud which disguised their flat, level bottoms and vertical sides, there was no doubting that they were the remnants of peat extraction on an industrial scale. Even so, there are still some who think they know better...

2 Climate, vegetation and wildlife

Above: Weather vane at South Walsham
Opposite: Ragged robin and yellow rattle, Strumpshaw Fen

The 1854 edition of Francis White's *History, Gazetteer and Directory of Norfolk* describes the climate of Norfolk thus: 'Northerly and north-easterly winds prevail more in Norfolk than in any other part of the kingdom; vegetation is consequently seriously retarded in the spring. Rains are more frequent during the summer months than in the midland counties; and are occasioned by vapours from Holland, and by the contiguity of the sea, and of the Lincolnshire and Cambridgeshire marshes.'

But while the climate of the Broads had been described during the reign of James I as 'pleasant for habitation – good, sweet, and where the air is delectable', it would seem that the average Victorian at the time of the Crimean War had rather less to get excited about. White again: 'In Marshland Hundred, and other fenny districts, it is exceedingly damp, and subjects the inhabitants to intermittent fevers: but the fens and marshes are now to a great extent drained, so that these endemical agues are much less frequent than formerly.'

The Broads, along with the rest of Norfolk, is in fact the driest part of Britain, with weather which tends to be rather more Continental than the rest of the country. That is simply because Norfolk is at the most easterly edge of the widest point of Britain, and given that the prevailing wind comes from the west across the Atlantic, most of the rain has already been shed on Ireland and western England by the time it arrives here. According to Met Office figures for the long-term average 1961–90, rainfall in East Anglia amounts to approximately 23½in (600mm) per year, which is around a third of what you would expect in the Lake District, the wettest part of the country. The driest month is actually February. When it comes to the number of hours of sunshine per

day, Norfolk is only a shade (if you'll excuse the pun) behind Cornwall, the top-scoring county in the country. May is the sunniest month, when Norfolk boasts over 200 hours of sunshine.

Generally speaking the range between the lowest and highest temperatures, both seasonally and on a daily basis, is much greater here than it is on the western side of the country. Having said that, the proximity of the North Sea – or German Ocean, as it used to be known – tends to be a moderating influence on the weather in areas closest to the coast, and that includes the Broads. When temperatures further inland are plummeting, it is quite likely that the Broads will be a degree or so warmer. The summer will see a relatively high incidence of thunderstorms and showers, while in the spring, the sea's slowness to warm up will often add a chill to any wind coming in from the east or north. The fact that the counties of Norfolk and Suffolk bulge out into the North Sea means that when winds do come in from those directions they will bring a higher risk of rain than they would in other parts of the country.

There can be some marked variations in the weather over just a few miles when the conditions are right. In the late spring and early summer, light easterly winds can often result in what north of the Border they would call a 'haar' – coastal fog formed where the cooler air coming in off the sea meets the warmer air rising off the land. It's quite possible to be wandering among the sand dunes at Winterton, or at Hickling Broad just inland, feeling decidedly chilly and with not much visibility, while just a few miles further inland, Horning and Wroxham will be bathed in warm sunshine.

During the winter it is quite often the case that when it is really bitterly cold and freezing in Cambridgeshire, it will be somewhat milder in the Broads, where wind coming off the sea will still be picking up any residual warmth from the summer. But while there is less precipitation, winters can still be pretty hard. Any wind sweeping directly from the north has absolutely no land to pass over between Norfolk and the polar ice cap, so when it gets cold, it does so with a biting vengeance. Indeed, occasional extremes of cold have left the broads and rivers ice-bound, frozen solid enough for the more adventurous to strap on their ice skates and travel for miles on the glassy surface.

In fact, up until around 100 years ago, any ice which did form in the winter months would be scooped up and stored in the many ice houses around the region. Of course, for an area which depended on a trade in fish, having the means to store it was essential before mechanised refrigeration, and when the winters were too mild to produce the ice on our doorstep it had to be imported from as far afield as Scandinavia.

NATURE CONSERVATION

Norfolk is very much the home of nature conservation in Britain. The county was the first to institute a naturalist's trust, in 1926, these days known as the Norfolk Wildlife Trust, with nearly forty sites throughout the county in its care. Of course some of those are in the Broads, and indeed, the value of the Broads

Above: Floating conservation centre, Ranworth
Opposite: Marsh mallow, Halvergate
Below: Yellow flag iris on Strumpshaw Fen

vegetation and wildlife can be no better underlined than by the rich concentration of nature conservation sites. There are six National Nature Reserves, and twenty-seven Sites of Special Scientific Interest located wholly or partially in the Broads. And while they represent the most important sites, they are very much dependent on the survival of the surrounding areas as their 'buffer zones'.

The Broads are unique in Britain as a wetland ecosystem, and within that are a number of component parts: the rivers and broads themselves; the surrounding fens and woodlands; the drained marshlands towards the coast, and the estuary habitat provided by Breydon Water. Each has its own distinct character and wildlife although, inevitably, there is a certain amount of crossover.

RIVERS AND BROADS

Some of the broads are directly associated with the main rivers of the region – the Bure, Ant, Thurne, Yare and Waveney – while others are completely isolated. The water is mostly fresh, and calcareous on account of its origins in the underlying chalk. The Thurne broads, however, are close enough to the coast for the water to be brackish, and so their flora and fauna are somewhat different.

Before the pressures of boating, agriculture, and the needs of an increasing (and encroaching) population, the broads would have been smothered in water-lilies and arrowhead, while beneath the surface plants like water soldier would have thrived, providing a marvellous habitat for fish and wildfowl. Many factors have combined to reduce the quality of the water over the years, and as a result the main waterways of the Broads are not the magnificent havens of flora and fauna they once were. The problems are being addressed by the Broads Authority, and they have enjoyed some marked successes in bringing broads such as Cockshoot and Barton back to life, as well as taking measures to improve the situation generally throughout the area.

Even so, the Broads waters contain a wider variety of freshwater fish species than can be found in rivers on the western side of the country, and are famous for their pike; perch, bream, dace and roach are also common.

Just about the commonest bird you are likely to see swimming on open water is the coot, easily recognised by its dull, velvety black feathers and white bill. Coots build floating nests at the water's edge, and feed on water weeds, although they can often be seen on land, nibbling grass. Without doubt one of the more distinctive visitors to the larger stretches of open water in the Broads is the great crested grebe. Immediately recognisable by their black-and-chestnut tufted crests, they can often be seen in the early summer swimming about with their young perched on their backs.

One mammal making something of a comeback in the Broads is the common otter, due in no small part to the efforts of the Otter Trust at Earsham, near Bungay. Over the last twenty years it has operated a programme of releases into the wild, bringing the species back from virtual extinction. Up until the 1950s otters had been plentiful, and although some have surmised that their rapid decline was due to the destruction of habitats through increased boating, the underlying cause was found to be the level of pollution in the water.

BIRDS OF THE BROADS

These days the elusive bittern – a type of heron – is perhaps the best reminder of the fragility of the Broads' ecosystem. By 1850 bitterns had ceased to breed in Britain, victims to both marsh drainage and shooting. Fifty years later they had managed to re-establish themselves in the reedbeds of the broads. But since then pressures on habitats and deteriorating water quality have seen their numbers decline once more. Today's population of bitterns in the Broads is very small – fewer than twenty – and if you happen to see one you can count yourself very lucky indeed.

Around 30in (76cm) long, the bittern has buff plumage, streaked with brown, and green feet and legs. It stalks the reedbeds in a characteristic hunch-backed manner, and is rarely seen beyond

Continued on page 37

FENS AND WOODLANDS

At the edges of the broads and rivers are boggy areas called fens. These water-logged fringes, thick with reed and sedge, are home to over 250 different species of plant, and in many cases, unique to this part of Britain. The list numbers several species of orchid, including the yellowish green-flowered fen orchid, protected under the Wildlife and Countryside Act 1981.

During the summer the water's edge gains shades of pink and purple, with hemp agrimony, great willowherb and purple loosestrife. Many species of umbellifer (like cow parsley) can be found, including abundant milk parsley, which is scarce elsewhere. It is for this reason that the beautiful swallowtail butterfly, Britain's largest, can only be found in the Broads, particularly around Hickling and How Hill, where there are plentiful shoots of milk parsley, on which the swallowtail lays its eggs. The first swallowtails emerge on sunny May days, drying their wings as they bask on the reeds. Not very easy to find (unless you know what you are looking for), swallowtails are nevertheless unmistakable when you do come across them, their bodies and wings a riot of black and gold, with iridescent flashes of blue and red. Other distinctive species include dragonflies and damselflies, skitting across the water, and the Norfolk hawker, a type of dragonfly unique to the area, and adopted by the Broads Authority as its emblem.

Continued from page 36
the reeds in open water. If disturbed, it freezes with its neck and bill pointing upwards, doing its best to merge into the surrounding reeds. Its most distinguishing feature without doubt is its hollow, booming call. Heard in the breeding season in early summer, it resembles something between a cow and a foghorn. An uncommon sight in the summer, your best chance of seeing one is more likely during winter, when they fly low, just above the reeds.

The Marsh Harrier is a large, broad-winged bird of prey that lays its eggs on a thick platform of vegetation in the densest parts of the reedbeds, and consequently its breeding grounds in Britain are confined to East Anglia. It too suffered at the hands of gameshooters, but it has made something of a comeback. Flying low and steady just above the reedbeds, it makes frequent extended glides, holding its wings stiffly in a shallow 'V', on the lookout for small birds, and mammals such as voles.

Also known as the reedling, the bearded tit is dependent on large reedbeds for both feeding and breeding. The male is predominantly chestnut brown with pale buff underparts, and a dove-grey head. Most characteristic are the black streaks on either side of its white throat, producing a comical sort of 'sergeant-major's moustache' effect.

Opposite above: Heron at Horning
Above: Mallards at Ranworth
Left: Marsh orchid, reed mace, king cup

Above: Insect life, Cockshoot
Right: Boardwalk sign, Ranworth
Opposite: Dog rose, Strumpshaw Fen

The fens represent the first stage in a natural process called succession, where the open water becomes woodland over a period of time. Mud and dead vegetation accumulate low down in the water. Because it is not so well oxygenated here, decomposition is minimal and peat forms, and the water becomes shallow enough for reeds to take root. Ultimately, scrub trees known as 'carr' take a hold in the reedbed, drying out the land further. Unchecked, the transition from reedbed to woodland can take place in as little as twenty years, the reason why a certain level of management, in the form of reed-cutting, is essential to preserve the status quo. A good place to see the effects of succession is at Ranworth, where a boardwalk nature trail to the visitor centre – a building floating on pontoons on the broad itself – explains the various stages along the way. Without the boardwalk, it would be impossible to visit this part of the Broads, since the terrain is wet and positively glutinous – challenging to say the least.

The final stage in the relatively quick process of succession is carr woodland, after which the more long-term development of oak and ash woodland takes place. Probably the closest thing we have in Britain to an impenetrable jungle, mature carr woodland of alder, birch and sallow trees, and shrubs like blackthorn, dog rose and brambles, provides a damp and shady environment in which ferns, mosses and lichens can thrive.

Apart from supporting many common species of woodland birds, you can also expect to see greater and lesser spotted woodpeckers, treecreepers and long-tailed tits, all making good use of the abundant supply of seeds, fruits and insects. It's not just the ecological value which makes the fens and carr woodland such vital components of the Broads. They also do a rather fine job of blurring the edges between the water and land environments, and adding an element of scale as well.

NOT WHAT YOU'D EXPECT...

The woodlands of the Broads provide an unlikely home for one particularly unexpected mammal – the Chinese water deer. Nobody is certain how they came to be here, since the nearest wildlife park with such animals is far enough away to make their escape and migration extremely improbable. It seems more likely that they were privately kept in captivity in the Horning area during the 1950s, and that some may have escaped. Although they prefer to hide away in thick undergrowth and trees, Chinese water deer feed mainly on grass shoots and other small plants, so their introduction to the Broads has had no significant ecological impact.

The other foreign species which established itself here did, however, make considerably more of a mark. The coypu is a large aquatic rodent, a native of South America, brought over to Britain in the late 1920s and early 1930s to be bred for its dense fur. Inevitably there were escapes, and when all the coypu farms were closed down at the beginning of World War II, more coypus escaped into the wild. Two major populations established in Britain, one in the Broads, and over the next twenty years or so they did a considerable amount of damage to reedbeds, and consequently to river banks. For many years the numbers were held in check by trapping, until the decision to eradicate them entirely. Although there have been odd reported sightings since, coypus were declared to have been wiped out by the end of the 1980s.

DRAINED MARSHLANDS

The eastern Broads landscape is very much dominated by drained marshlands. For hundreds of years people have attempted to improve the drainage of the flat, low-lying, boggy land between Norwich and Great Yarmouth in order to graze livestock, and we can perhaps be thankful that it was not carried out with the all-consuming zeal with which the Earl of Bedford drained the marshes of the Cambridgeshire and Lincolnshire Fens in the seventeenth century.

Even so, ditches (or dykes, as they are known locally) were being dug as far back as the fourteenth century to help drain the land and protect it from

flooding, and by the end of the eighteenth century they had been augmented by numerous wind-powered drainage pumps. The regime which developed was one which allowed grazing during the summer months, the drainage pumps being capable of scooping sufficient water out of the dykes and pumping it into the rivers. In fact, the dykes were multi-functional. Not only did they provide the all-important means of drainage, they were also a source of drinking water for the cattle being fattened for market, and also prevented them from straying onto adjacent marshes. During the winter months the land would be allowed to flood, so providing further prime spots for passing wildfowl and waders.

Above: Rose hips, Horsey Mere
Pages 42–3: Haddiscoe New Cut

The dykes are great havens for a wide variety of plants and wildlife, many of which would originally have been much more widespread throughout the broads, when overall water quality was far higher. They include many species of pondweed, water violet and greater bladderwort. But even throughout the dyke system of the drained marshlands the water varies from freshwater to brackish, depending on the amount of seepage from nearby tidal waters; as a result the plantlife in each system of dykes will vary, the brackish waters supporting plants like fennel-leaved pondweed and sea club-rush.

The grazing marshes are wonderful places for spotting birds. In the summer you can delight to the musical song of skylarks, abundant in areas like this with low-intensity farmed grasslands, but becoming scarce elsewhere. Take a walk beside a marsh dyke, and the chances are you'll spot a heron standing motionless at the water's edge, waiting for that moment to take a fish. Known in Norfolk as 'harnsers', around 100 breed in the Broads every year, and the young birds come to the marsh dykes to feed. On the marshes themselves you can expect to see nesting oystercatchers, redshank and lapwing.

The Broads is now designated an Environmentally Sensitive Area, which not only recognises the vital importance of its ecosystems, but also provides financial support for the farmers to ensure the continuation of the traditional grazing regime upon which the marshes rely. The story behind what nearly happened to the marshes at Halvergate and the surrounding area is explored further in Chapter 3.

ESTUARY

The only estuary habitat in the Broads is Breydon Water, the wild and lonely expanse of tidal water inland from Great Yarmouth, all that is left of the once-mighty combined outfall of the Broads rivers of the Roman era. It is also unique in that it is Britain's most easterly estuary. Here, when the tide is out, vast mud-flats play host to numerous migrating birds, but also to a variety of species that come to spend the winter. Shelduck, with its characteristic bulbous red knob at the top of its bill, can be seen here, along with Bewick's swans, wigeons, gold-eneyes and pink-footed geese. In late summer you can expect to see waders like black-tailed godwits and avocets, as well as dunlin and plover. Cormorants come here in large numbers, and can often be seen sitting on the wooden posts at the water's edge with their wings outstretched. Their feathers are not very waterproof, so after each dive into the water to take some fish – and they eat several times their own weight in a day – they need to dry them out.

Birdwatchers, equipped with binoculars and cameras with long lenses, may be seen around the fringes of Breydon at any time of year. In fact Breydon was one of the very first nature reserves in the country, dating back to the formation of the Breydon Wild Birds Protection Society in 1888, brought about in response to the increasing damage to flocks being wrought by wildfowlers. Today the greater part of Breydon Water is looked after by the Royal Society for the Protection of Birds.

Right: Greylag geese, Hickling

3 Man's influence

The Broads have long been recognised as an area of outstanding importance. They were even mooted as a National Park along with the first areas for consideration back in the late 1940s. Julian Huxley wrote that he couldn't imagine a system of National Parks in Britain which didn't include the Norfolk Broads.

So what happened? Why did the Broads fail to make the original National Park line-up? The real problem was the fact that the pressures and needs in the Broads were quite different from those of the upland areas being considered at the time. While the upland areas were all about wilderness and open space, the Broads was a wetland area being threatened by intensive agriculture.

The Nature Conservancy Council (now English Nature) started to make warning noises in the mid-sixties about the decline of nature conservation in the area, but it wasn't until a decade or so later that the Countryside Commission warned that unless the local authorities found some good method of managing the Broads, they would exercise their mandatory powers to designate it a National Park.

So it was that the original Broads Authority came into being in 1979, founded by eight partners: Suffolk and Norfolk County Councils; the two urban councils of Great Yarmouth and Norwich; and the district councils of North and South Norfolk, Broadland and Wavency. They tied in with the Anglian Water Authority (now Anglian Water), and the navigation body, the Great Yarmouth Port and Haven Commissioners. Curiously, the Nature Conservancy Council, the body which had sounded the alarm in the first place, chose to remain at a distance. The new authority's first priority was to set up working groups to look at the various problem areas: ecology, landscape and recreation. Three main problems emerged: the quality of the water, the threat of draining the marshlands, and pressures from the numbers of boats.

WATER

Back in the days when Victorians and Edwardians came to holiday on the Broads, the water quality was beyond compare. You can see it in some of the early photographs taken by the likes of P.H. Emerson: beautiful water-lilies cover the surface, and there are abundant reeds at the water's edge. By the latter half of the twentieth century, the increase in population and in intensive agriculture was starting to take its toll. So what was the problem?

Phosphates, which come from treated sewage effluent and things like washing-up liquid, were getting into the sewage outfalls, and intensive farming meant that nitrates from fertilisers were running off into the river system. When the phosphates and nitrates came together, it was not so much that the water had become polluted, but enriched. It caused a pea-soup-like algal explosion, clouding the water and shading out the plants which depend on sunlight. With plants no longer anchoring the

Left: Duck weed and reeds, How Hill estate

Above: Algae warning, Filby Broad

bottoms of the rivers and broads, erosion occurred at a much faster rate.

Eutrophication – this over-enrichment of the water – is exacerbated when warm summers and low water levels combine to promote the growth of blue-green algae, which is highly toxic and a health hazard to anyone coming into contact with it. But there was more. Agricultural pollution from discharges of silage liquor is vastly more damaging than domestic water, as its high ammonia content is extremely toxic. And there is the legacy of industrial pollution from the 1960s, when high levels of mercury were discharged at various points into the River Yare.

Dredging of the river bed, necessary to maintain navigation, stirs up the mercury compounds and threatens the wildlife. Badly maintained motor boats may allow oil to leak into bilge water, which is then pumped out into the environment. This is not a problem with hire boats – these have a self-regulating system which ensures oily water is not pumped out – but it is with privately owned vessels.

While everyone had expected instantaneous results from the fledgling Broads Authority, its first action was to spend around half a million pounds on research – a lot of money for such a small authority – and various experimental management projects. The ecology group had come to the conclusion that while the nitrate problem was too difficult to tackle, simply because the sources were too diverse and widely spread, it ought to be possible to combat the water-quality problem by reducing the amount of phosphates in the water.

Phosphates were getting into the river system via the various sewage treatment works, so one idea was to persuade the Anglian Water Authority to add controlled quantities of ferric sulphate to the sewage effluent to neutralise them. This chemical stripping process removes over 90 per cent of the phosphates. In recent years this has been augmented by sophisticated sand filters which remove particulate phosphorus.

Ten years after phosphate stripping began at sewage treatment works on the Upper Bure and Ant, however, the recovery was not as dramatic as had been hoped. The problem was that the mud at the bottoms of the broads was also rich in nutrients.

So the next, more ambitious, plan involved Cockshoot Broad, a broad of around 9 acres (3.6ha) on the other side of the River Bure from Horning, near Woodbastwick. It had silted up so much that mud lay only a couple of inches below the surface. The mud contained the legacy of phosphate, which bubbled out every spring. The Broads Authority dammed the broad off so it couldn't be further enriched, and then used a suction dredger to pump out about 4ft (1.2m) of mud, roughly equivalent to forty-four full Olympic-sized swimming pools.

Within two to three months seeds which had lain dormant at the bottom of the broad for almost forty years started to germinate. They also transplanted water plants from other broads and marsh dykes to help kick-start the system. Cockshoot Broad is clear now, and the surface of Cockshoot Dyke is peppered with broad lily pads, demonstrating nature's power of recovery – given the right conditions.

Below: Plant cages, Ranworth Broad. One with and one without a wire cover, to see if birds are causing a problem

A PEACEFUL EXPLORATION

Without doubt, the best way to appreciate the restoration of Barton Broad is by taking a trip on Britain's first solar-powered passenger-carrying electric boat, the Ra. Built in Germany from stainless steel, this unusual boat looks like a high-tech entry for a raft race, with twin pontoons and a roof consisting of three banks of seven solar panels. She can carry up to a dozen people at a time, and is tall enough to allow passengers the rare opportunity to look out over the reedbeds. With her very quiet twin electric motors, the Ra is the ideal way to appreciate the broad and its wildlife.

Other suction-dredging projects have taken place at a number of sites, and a technique called bio-manipulation has been used afterwards to help clear the waters of algae. It involves temporarily removing fish from the food chain by stunning them with an electric current and moving them to another area. With fewer predators, water fleas can thrive. They have a prodigious appetite for algae and, providing there are no fish feeding on them will happily munch their way through the algae and clear the water.

This technique has been used in the Broads Authority's biggest project to date, Clear Water 2000, the name given to the restoration of Barton Broad, the second largest. A huge amount of mud was pumped from the bottom of the broad, and piped into adjacent settlement lagoons where it was left to dry out before being spread on nearby fields. The fish were removed and water fleas released into the broad to chomp their way through the algae. Funded not just by the Broads Authority and Environment Agency, the project received a major grant from the Millennium Commission, along with other funding from Anglian Water, the Soap and Detergent Industry's Environmental Trust, and Norfolk Environmental Waste Services. The project also involved constructing land access to the broad in the form of a public walkway.

MARSH DRAINAGE – THE HALVERGATE SAGA

The grazing marshes inland from Great Yarmouth are particularly important, not just for their unique landscape value, but because of the fragile ecology of the dykes which criss-cross the fields. In many cases they're the last reservoirs of plantlife that used to exist throughout the broads before they started to deteriorate.

The traditional regime had always involved the grazing of cattle, but from the 1960s onwards, MAFF, the Ministry of Agriculture Fisheries and Food, started a relentless drive towards turning the marshes over to growing cereal crops. A generation on from the end of World War II, production was very much the order of the day, and grants were available to farmers to take up schemes offered by the Internal Drainage Boards to lower the water table and plough up the fields. It was certainly going to be a lot more profitable to convert to cereal production than continue with cattle grazing, which had become a pretty marginal business.

The situation came to a head in the early to mid-1980s, by which time many hundreds of acres of marshland had already fallen under the plough. The newspaper headline writers had their own field day. According to them,

Left: Halvergate Marshes

the evil farmers were draining the Broads for profit, and for what? To provide cereal which qualified for grants under the EEC's lunatic Common Agricultural Policy – cereal which would simply end up in a vast shed, part of the EEC grain mountain.

MAFF were in something of a Catch 22 situation. The newly formed Broads Authority was asking them to protect the area, but their remit was one of production. So first the Broads Authority tried to see if the EEC's directives on less favoured areas, already operating in the Isles of Scilly, could be interpreted to the Broads position. Unfortunately MAFF proved to be reluctant on that point: hardly surprising, when you tried to imply that the Broads, an area in intensive agricultural production, was handicapped.

But out of that MAFF achieved a change in the EEC structural directives, allowing them for the first time ever to make payments for conservation purposes. The Broads Grazing Marsh Conservation Scheme broke the mould. The Broads Authority expected a 30 to 40 per cent take-up, and were more than pleasantly surprised to find nearly 90 per cent of the farmers approached taking up the offer of £50 per acre per year to continue with traditional grazing, rather than going for profit with cereal, as they could have done. In fact the only farmers who did not take up the scheme were those absentee landlords which the Authority could not trace.

So the Grazing Marsh Scheme became the catalyst which provided the model for Environmentally Sensitive Areas, and the Broads in their entirety were subsequently designated an ESA in July 1986.

BOATS – TOURISM PRESSURES

The third major problem was the pressure of boat numbers. When this problem was at its height, there were more boats on the Broads than on any other waterway system in Europe. Over the last twenty years those numbers have reduced simply by the action of market forces: boating holidays on the Broads are not as popular as they once were. Nevertheless, during the early eighties, the initial call was to go to Government and ask for legislation controlling boat numbers, but that would have been totally impractical. Just as every person has a basic right to drive a car on the road, every navigational interest in the country would have opposed the idea.

Instead, the Broads Authority suggested that the Broads – both land and water space – should be managed by one authority. It was highly controversial at the time, not least because it looked as though it was slighting the navigation authority, one of their partners who had been with them all along. But as a result of this, legislation was passed to give the Broads National Park status, and likewise the Broads Authority the status of a National Park Authority.

A healthy river bank has a gently sloping rond – a beach, if you like – fronted by reeds. This natural cushion helps protect the bank against wave action. The problem, exacerbated by the eutrophication process which was causing a decline in the reeds, was the fact that motor boats produced considerably more damaging wash than natural wave action. The effect is to undermine the vegetation at the edge of the river, and ultimately eat into the bank itself. That in turn means that dredging will be required elsewhere in the river system, since all the eroded material ends up as sediment somewhere.

Right: Bank erosion, Salhouse Broad

PLEASE DON'T HURRY...

One fairly straightforward solution to reduce bank erosion, introduced early on, was to institute speed limits. The Broads Authority found that between 4 and 7mph, each 1mph increase strengthened the wave energy hitting the river bank by a factor of 3.4. In 1992 they instituted a range of new lower speed limits throughout the Broads, the maximums depending on the vulnerability of the river banks.

The lower reaches of the Waveney, Yare and Bure are set at 6mph, while further upstream and in more sensitive areas, the limit is as low as 3mph. Signs on the river banks warn boat users to reduce their speed, and Broads Authority River Inspectors enforce the limits. Boat-hire companies are also provided with information to pass on to their clients, explaining the purpose of the speed limits.

Above: Plastic matting to encourage bank plants and stability
Opposite: Electric fleet, Potter Heigham

One solution is to protect the river bank using sheet-steel or timber piling, but it is extremely expensive, and the result is far from ideal. It looks unattractive, more akin to a canal than a river bank, is susceptible to damage, and offers no means for reeds and other vegetation to grow back. A number of alternatives have been tried, including using wire cages filled with stones, and open-cell concrete blockwork.

Solutions such as these look unsightly at first, but in time are colonised by plants which softens their appearance. Geotextile matting is used on river banks where the wash is not so extreme. The matting is laid like a carpet, following the contours of the river bank, and plants then grow through its open weave. This stabilises the bank whilst retaining its natural look. Other more natural solutions include coir rolls – matting made from biodegradable coconut fibres – and piling made from alder poles, visually more acceptable than steel or concrete, and locally available in abundance. In general, the policy is to protect river banks using more natural methods, and only to employ piling where these prove to be impracticable.

Something else which is being investigated is the idea of wash-free zones. Rather than a speed limit as such, boat users would simply be expected not to produce any significant wash in these areas, whatever their speed. This would protect particularly vulnerable banks, and it also reminds the boat-builders and hirers that they too can contribute to the conservation of the Broads. The traditional Broads motor cruiser was built with comfort and amenity the main consideration, and as the overall visual impact of such boats was never considered, neither were the effects of wash; it simply did not enter into the equation.

Research by the Broads Authority showed that the shape of the hull was critical to the level of wash generated. The short stubby bows of cruisers built in the 1970s were the worst offenders, producing large waves as they punched through the water. By contrast, longer, sleeker hulls were shown to produce much less powerful waves. In fact, they also showed that the traditional hull designs were far more environmentally friendly than the so-called modern ones. So much for progress!

The builders and hirers have accepted the principle but, of course, translating that into practice is fraught with drawbacks, given the amount of investment required, and the downturn in boating holidays on the Broads generally. Even so, many of the new hire boats on the Broads are built with the latest low-wash hulls.

But while the motor cruisers are gradually working towards more environmentally friendly hulls, another class of boat with big potential to cause problems is day-hire boats. As with the overall boat-hire industry, the numbers have declined somewhat over the last twenty years due to market forces, but many of the day boats on the Broads have poor wash characteristics, made worse by the fact that they are often driven by people intent on covering as much ground as possible within their day's hiring. Many day-boat-hire companies banded together to form their own association, bringing in a voluntary 5mph speed restriction on their boats; and the Broads Authority has encouraged them by ensuring they provide hirers with realistic information about the distances they can expect to cover within their hire time.

Apart from encouraging the introduction of day boats with low-wash hulls, the latest most exciting development is electrically powered day boats. The limitations of the power source means that the hulls are much more likely to have been constructed with the greatest efficiency in mind, which in turn means low wash. Recharged overnight, electric day boats are not only environmentally friendly, their quietness also makes them ideal for those who want to appreciate the peace of the Broads, and get closer to the wildlife.

Perhaps the Holy Grail in Broads cruisers would be the introduction of electrically powered craft for weekly hire. That in itself is fraught with problems. While battery technology has improved substantially over the last few years, most boat hirers do not feel it has progressed far enough to make electrically powered cruisers viable. And of course the infrastructure in terms of moorings with recharging points needs to be in place as well. However, that particular situation is being addressed.

The bottom line, as far as motor boats is concerned, is that they are not encouraged. And while their numbers cannot be controlled directly, the Broads Authority can limit them indirectly with its planning powers: if, for example, a boatyard wanted to build an extension in order to accommodate more boats. Having said that, the hire-boat industry is recognised as an important contributor to the local economy, so the balance is still very delicate.

THE BUILT ENVIRONMENT

Take a look at the buildings in other National Parks, and you may detect an underlying theme, which could well relate to the way the local stone is used. In the Broads, no single style of building predominates. Out in the marshes, it is the windpumps which catch the eye.

Opposite above: Moorings near Postwick (pronounced Pozzick), River Yare
Opposite below: Boat hire station, Wroxham
Below: Waterside thatched property, River Bure

Above and below: Holiday homes, River Thurne near Potter Heigham

Once there were well over 200; now only around seventy survive. The old settlements, generally consisting of a few houses and cottages grouped around the village common, or next to the staithe, have a natural scale as befits the area. More modern buildings on the Broads include everything from quaint riverside chalets and traditional boat houses to large dwellings, some of which fit in with their surroundings better than others. Then there are the commercial buildings which include the boatyards and tourist developments, which have certainly done nothing for the character and appearance of places such as Wroxham and Hoveton.

In the boom-and-bust years of the 1980s, many boatyards felt the pinch and had to face making changes or going out of business. Several decided the way to do it would be by redeveloping. Prime riverside sites were at a premium, and the opportunity to pull down boat sheds and replace them with lucrative holiday accommodation proved irresistible. But in some cases where the redevelopments went through unchecked, the result was unattractive buildings which did not blend in with their environment. Today if a boatyard owner looks to some kind of redevelopment, the all-important concern is that the employment aspect should be retained, and that there is no loss of amenity as far as water users are concerned.

In all cases now, the Broads Authority's concern is to make sure that those buildings which need protection get it, even if it means some kind of change in use. Certainly it is better to retain the important features rather than see them suffer at the hands of unsympathetic development. And when it comes to saving important buildings, the means can sometimes be quite drastic. A Victorian summerhouse at May Gurney's dockyard at Thorpe, dating back to 1860 and lived in by three generations of dockyard workers, was relocated some 200yd (180m) down the river in order to save it from flooding.

If there is one over-riding aspect which has been proved in the Broads, it is that with very complex and conflicting interests, and indeed complicated and diverse problems in the area, solutions can be found – both technically, and administratively. And that is something of which the Broads Authority can be justly proud.

Below: Riverside houses, Horning, River Bure

4 Land use, culture and customs

The Broads has always been very much a working landscape. Over the centuries, they have provided virtually every basic need for man's survival: peat for fuel, reed and sedge for thatched roofs, hay from the marshes for cattle, fish and wildfowl for food.

Today's land uses are somewhat more diverse. As a National Park, the Broads needs to maintain a delicate balance between agriculture, tourism and conservation. It is important that the area has a healthy economy, but not at the expense of the beautiful landscape and rich wildlife. It is that balancing act which the Broads Authority has to carry out, with great skill and understanding of all the issues involved. It undertakes conservation work where necessary, and provides a framework of encouragement to promote good practices which enhance both the protection and our enjoyment of the Broads.

Top: Tunstead Trosh
Above: Sugar beet, Sharp Street
Right: Grazing marshes, Beccles

AGRICULTURE

Ever since man has lived in the Broads, the land and water have provided for his needs. In terms of farming, the biggest factor has been the rich grazing afforded by the flat marshlands on the lower reaches of the Broads rivers, roughly occupying the triangle between Norwich, Beccles and Great Yarmouth.

Cattle would be driven down from Scotland, then fattened up on the marshes before finally going to market, either locally in Norwich or Great Yarmouth, or at Smithfield in London. Daniel Defoe commented on the way these 'Scots runts' grew 'monstrously fat, and the beef is so delicious that the inhabitants prefer them to the English cattle'.

Elsewhere in the county, agriculture involved extensive sheep grazing and arable crops, and it was in this latter that the famous agriculturalist Thomas Coke of Holkham, Norfolk, was highly influential in the late eighteenth and

Above: Free range pigs, Salhouse
Opposite top: Thatching at Hickling
Opposite below: Eel-fishing, Candle Dyke

early nineteenth centuries. Among many other innovations he also pioneered the practice of crop rotation, interspersing plantings of corn with fodder crops and a period lying fallow. Around the Broads, agriculture had traditionally involved the grazing of cattle, but as windpumps were replaced by steam-driven ones, then later by diesel engines and finally electric pumps, farmers looked at the means to lower the water table permanently as an opportunity to 'improve' marshland drainage and convert to growing cereals, spurred on by grants from the Ministry of Agriculture.

This practice, examined in further detail in the preceding chapter, came to a head in the 1980s, when the threat that drainage posed to the unique ecology of the marshlands was exposed. The fledgling Broads Authority proposed a scheme which encouraged farmers to maintain the traditional grazing regime, aided by Government-funded grants.

REED-CUTTING

If there is one activity which demonstrates how a certain level of management is essential for conservation, it is reed-cutting. Over the centuries, the prime motive has been the fact that the reeds are exceptionally versatile: not only are they the best material available for thatching roofs, they also have many other uses, including basket-making. If it wasn't for this demand, the shape (and indeed size) of the broads would be considerably different, because cutting the reedbeds on a regular basis is essential to prevent succession – the process whereby the watery margins of the broads and dykes turn into carr woodland – taking over.

Before mechanisation, the reed-cutters would have to stand in up to a foot of water, using a long-handled scythe to swish into the reeds. The job would be done in winter so the reeds would be more or less bare-stemmed and devoid of leaves and, once cut, any remaining loose bits would be removed and they would be tied up into bundles called shooves. On average, it would take about 2,000 shooves to roof a house.

In many cases the most plentiful reeds would grow a long way from any road, or even from ground dry enough for a horse and cart. So they would be piled up onto a reed lighter – a flat-bottomed boat – which, depending on its size, would either be towed or 'quanted' (see page 67) to the nearest staithe. There the bundles would be offloaded, in the old days ready to be transported by wherry, latterly by road. These days the vast majority of reed-cutting is carried out using something more akin to a motor mower – a modified rice harvester which not only cuts the reeds but bundles them up into shooves as well.

FISHING

As the peat pits became unworkable with rising water levels, it was inevitable that people in the Broads would turn to other means to support themselves, and fishing was one obvious choice: water was abundant – and so were fish.

Eels used to be caught by various means, including simply stringing nets across a river, or using fyke nets – traps made of netting on a series of hoops. Fyke nets still survive, and although eel-fishing no longer continues on the

same scale, licences are still issued, and many of the eels that are caught are exported to Holland. The last traditional eel sett which continues to function is at Candle Dyke. These days fishing has become more of a recreational than commercial activity, and coarse fishing is extremely popular in the Broads.

WILDFOWLING

Shooting ducks for the table, and rarer fowl for wealthy collectors to have stuffed, was very much a preoccupation in Victorian times and the early part of the twentieth century. The guns used by wildfowlers were specially made with extremely long barrels – measuring 8–9ft (2.4 – 2.7m) – and could not be fired unsupported. The wildfowler would use a specially constructed boat – a

KEEPING THE TRADITIONAL SKILLS ALIVE

The fact that the Broads is very much a managed landscape underlines the need to maintain those practices which keep the area looking the way we expect. Unless the reed banks which fringe the broads are cut back, those marshy margins will in time turn into carr woodland. Originally, of course, the reed was cut because it was a prime roofing material. Norfolk reed is still in demand for thatching – mainly because it will outlast a wheat thatch roof by a good forty years – but the prime requirement today is simply to cut the reed regularly for the purposes of management.

Once upon a time sons followed their fathers into the family trade, ensuring continuity in essential skills. These days, however, there are many other occupations to tempt young people, with the result that nobody is taking up reed-cutting. In the same way, the unique marshlands inland from Great Yarmouth remain the way they are because of the grazing regime. In the 1980s the practices which kept the grazing marshlands alive changed radically, and they were almost lost to modern agriculture. Now they are maintained through subsidies. Even so, we still need people who would rather tend stock than work in a burger bar in order to protect something that is not just a tradition, but an essential part of the fabric of the Broads.

A TOUGH WAY OF LIFE

The marshmen were, without doubt, the most versatile people to live in the Broads. Their occupations could well vary depending on the time of year, but would predominantly be involved with cattle grazing from spring through to autumn. Apart from tending the cattle, the marshman would have to ensure that the windpumps maintained the water on the marshes at the right level, with sufficient in the dykes to provide water for the cattle and to keep them from straying, but without flooding the pastures.

During the autumn, he would turn his hand to clearing the dykes of accumulated mud, and at the turn of the year would start cutting the reeds. Reed-cutting and thatching was also a significant part of the marshman's income, and the cutting would continue until the beginning of April, when the shoots of young reeds emerge from the water. He would also harvest sedge which, because it was more pliable, was better suited to covering the ridges of thatched houses. The marshman might also have had his own modest peat-digging, and take part in a spot of fishing or wildfowling; adaptability was the name of the game for these hardy folk living out in the isolation of the marshes.

This traditional way of life on the marshes died out gradually throughout the latter part of the nineteenth and the early twentieth centuries, as a result of the prohibition of drag fishing and wildfowling, and the introduction of more up-to-date methods of agriculture, combined with mechanised land drainage. A typical example of a marshman's cottage can be found at How Hill.

punt – with a draught of just a few inches, in which he would lie full length to keep a low profile, using a single oar to propel himself through the reeds. The idea was to get as close as possible to the birds before firing, doing so as they took flight. With his feet braced against the ribs of the boat to spread the load, the force of the recoil from the wildfowler's gun would be powerful enough to propel both punt and gunner backwards.

Wildfowling inevitably caused a high rate of attrition on birdlife in general, with what these days might be termed 'collateral damage' to other species. The large-scale killing of ducks and other wildfowl is now illegal.

WHERRIES – TRADITIONAL TRANSPORT BY WATER

Over the past 100 years, the *Albion*, with its distinctive black sail, has remained as our link with the days when up to 300 such graceful boats sailed up and down the rivers between Norwich and the coast. They carried all kinds of goods, from coal and timber to building supplies, ice, fish – in fact, everything that was needed to keep communities going.

It would be a two-way process, so goods for sale elsewhere – such as reeds for thatching – might go from some isolated Broads hamlet to Norwich, and the return journey would see the wherry's hold filled with horse manure to spread on the fields. Whatever the load, it would be piled in, or on, to excess. No journey was wasted.

The wherry was clinker-built (apart from the uniquely smooth-hulled carvel-built *Albion*), broad-beamed, but shallow in draft. Its mast was hinged and counterbalanced with an enormous 1½ ton lead weight, so that as little time as possible was spent when it came to negotiating the many low bridges which spanned the rivers. The black gaff sail – designed for maximum efficiency when the boat is passing close to trees on the banks – would come down, the mast would be lowered, and the wherry 'quanted' through. Generally crewed by just two people, the skipper and his mate, the hours were long and the work hard. Wherries were very fast, and capable of being sailed close to the wind, but when it refused to co-operate, or the boats needed to manoeuvre in tight spaces, 'quants' – hefty, 24ft (7.3m) long poles – would be used.

The advent of the railways spelled the beginning of the end for the wherries, and the final nail in the coffin was the development of improved roads throughout the area. The waterways were no longer the quickest means of transporting transport goods.

The *Albion* has for many years been the only surviving trading wherry afloat, often seen on the Broads doing recreational or educational excursions. Now she has been joined by *Maud*, a clinker-built vessel which survived until 1961, when she was sunk in Ranworth Broad along with several others to help protect the bank. She was raised in 1981 and then underwent a restoration which lasted very nearly twenty years.

WINDPUMPS

Perhaps more than anything else, windmills – which feature in so many paintings by members of the famous Norwich School of artists – characterise the Broads landscape. Of course, the low-lying land makes it well suited to mills, catching the winds which sweep in off the North Sea. Sutton Mill, near Stalham, is the tallest tower mill in the country, with nine floors, and a fascinating collection of old machinery and tools.

THE LAST PLEASURE WHERRIES

Of the surviving pleasure wherries, Hathor (pronounced 'Hartor', and built in 1905 for Ethel and Helen, daughters of mustard magnate Jeremiah Colman) is one of the finest. The interior follows an Egyptian theme as befits its name, with beautiful cabins and saloon panelled with sycamore and inlaid with teak Egyptian symbols. Now owned by the Wherry Yacht Charter, Hathor is a regular sight on the Broads, and is normally available for charter for families or groups up to a dozen.

In the summer, however, the Broads Authority charters Hartor and the wherry yachts Olive and Norada for a few weeks to do a sort of roadshow, touring the broads and making stopovers at various places to offer members of the public the opportunity to take short trips out to experience the unique delight of sailing in a large vessel on the Broads.

Above: Hathor *main cabin*
Left: Olive, Hathor *and* Norada, *three wherries on Wroxham Broad*

But on the whole most such structures were not built for grinding corn. While modern electric pumps regulate the water level of the marshy areas of the Broads, the original method used the power of the wind to turn scoop wheels. The surviving windpumps are attractive features of the countryside, and many have been restored to their former glory, preserving not just valuable landscape features, but important elements of industrial archaeology.

The windpumps at Stracey Arms, Berney Arms and Horsey – the last Broads windpump to be built, now in the care of the National Trust – are perhaps the more impressive, especially when you can climb up and appreciate the views. But you can hardly fail to be charmed by the open timber-framed trestle of Boardman's Mill at How Hill, or the pretty white-painted mill at Thurne Dyke. The latter is a prime example of a tower which has been 'hained', where the conical brick tower has been extended at the top with a cylindrical section to accommodate longer sails. As with many other Broads mills, the conversion came about with the invention of the patent self-regulating sail. Instead of common sails spread with canvas, the patent sail had shutters, and a mechanism to ensure that excessive gusts of wind did not add extra load on the system. At the same time, many windpumps were fitted with fantails, which ensured that the sails were kept pointed into the wind.

A TOUGH LIFE

Quanting a wherry was brutally hard work. With one end on the river bed, and the other to his shoulder, the crewman would lean on the quant and laboriously walk it the length of the wherry from bow to stern, then drag it back to start all over again. Calm days without wind were a wherryman's nightmare.

TOURISM

Tourism is a relatively recent addition to the catalogue of factors which have played a part in shaping the Broads. Around 150 years ago you would have thought of the broads and rivers in the kind of way that you'd view today's motorways. They were the means by which isolated communities kept in touch with larger towns and villages, and the means by which the articulated lorries of their day – black-sailed wherries – plied their trade.

The railways arrived in Norfolk in the mid-nineteenth century, not only making major inroads into the amount of waterborne goods carried, but also bringing in large numbers of people, pioneering the concept of holidays. The majority came to resorts like Great Yarmouth and Lowestoft, but some found their way inland to the Broads.

For a while, the trading wherries took on a double role, carrying cargoes in the winter and people in summer. In the beginning, the cargo holds would simply be cleaned out, perhaps one or two partitions erected, and hammocks slung inside. Somewhat basic, certainly, but without doubt an exciting adventure for anyone taking a break from a rather more mundane existence in the industrial Midlands. The Broads held a fascination for many Victorian visitors, simply through the way of life of the people who eked out a living here – the marshmen, eel-catchers, wherrymen and wildfowlers.

As the idea of coming to the Broads to holiday on the water took hold, so the facilities became more sophisticated. From the 1880s the white-sailed

Left: Boardman's Trestle Mill, River Ant

ANNUAL SERVICE

St Benet's Abbey, on the bank of the River Bure between the outfalls of the Rivers Ant and Thurne, traces its origins back to the time of King Canute. Over the centuries it built up its wealth and power until the dissolution of the monasteries in the reign of Henry VIII, when the monks departed, and much of the building became source material for other buildings, some as far away as Norwich. A windmill was built into the remaining walls of the gatehouse some 200 years ago, the ruins of which form the rather confused structure seen today. The abbot of St Benet's became Bishop of Norwich at the dissolution, and his successor, who holds both titles to this day, holds an open-air service at the ruins every year on the first Sunday in August, arriving at the abbey site by wherry.

Left: Hathor visitors' book, with H. Rider Haggard and Henry Wood's (Promenade Concerts) signatures, complete with musical stanza
Below: Wherry mechanics
Below left: The Bishop of Norwich on board the wherry Hathor en route for the annual outdoor service at St Benet's Abbey
Right: Wooden bridge, How Hill estate

pleasure wherry emerged, built with comfortable, fine panelled cabins instead of dark cargo holds, even equipped with pianos for that all-important evening entertainment. Gradually these evolved into wherry yachts, sleeker craft with even more refined interiors, and an afterdeck which gave the passengers somewhere to lounge and survey the passing scenery without interfering with the sailing of the boat.

John Loynes was a carpenter who built a boat for his own leisure on the Broads. The story goes that friends asked if he would hire it to them for their holiday, supposedly in 1878. That inspired him to set up a boat-hiring business, building more vessels to cater for the demand.

In the early days customers would collect their boat in Norwich and sail it round to Wroxham, where Loynes would have the smaller boats put on a horse-drawn cart to be taken back to Norwich, while the larger ones would be sailed back again ready for the next clients. By the early 1880s Loynes had set up a base for some of his boats in Wroxham, and by the end of the decade was operating a fleet of cabin cruisers fitted out with every convenience for self-contained holidays on the water.

By the turn of the century other companies were also operating boat hire on the Broads, and Loynes had diversified into international markets, setting up a yachting station in Friesland to cater for people looking to explore the waterways in Holland. Then along came Harry Blake. He'd taken a holiday with friends on a wherry yacht and decided to set up as a booking agent. His first modest brochure appeared in 1908, listing just the boats of Ernest Collins, with whom he had taken his holiday. The following year he added the boats of another dozen boatyards to his tally, and continued to expand from there.

The twenties and thirties saw the emergence of the motor cruiser, and once the Broads were opened to general navigation following a hiatus during the

Above: A foreigner (non-Broads), River Yare

war years, the biggest changes took place. For the first time, people had paid holidays, and mass-produced cars became affordable, so the numbers visiting the east-coast resorts and the Broads increased dramatically.

In the 1960s came one of the biggest developments to hit the boat-building industry – glass-fibre mouldings. This made it easier for boatyards to buy the hulls ready-made and simply fit them out. As a result, prices fell and hire fleets expanded. The numbers peaked in the 1970s, when motor cruisers for hire on the Broads numbered over 2,500.

In recent years the numbers of people holidaying in hire boats on the Broads has dropped, and some boatyards have gone out of business. This could be ascribed to today's holidaymakers wanting 'more sophisticated' holidays, although a lot has to do with the strength of sterling and the cheapness of holidays abroad compared with at home. And it must be said that many of the hire boats on the Broads are getting rather dated, and their replacement, not only on the grounds of marketability but also environmental factors (such as the tendency of the boats to create excessive wash and pollution), is long overdue. On the other side of the coin, the few remaining boat-builders who actually produce glass-fibre boats have progressed far beyond the technology of the average hire cruiser, and are now building boats for international markets.

While boating has to be the central core of any Broads holiday, tourism to the Broads has diversified far beyond that. With well over a million visitors a year, it is clear that a large number of people come not for two weeks on the water, but perhaps to tour the area from a central base, maybe taking a day boat one day, and a cycle ride the next. As such, it is not just the boat-hiring

agencies who benefit from tourism to the area. Accommodation – from hotels and bed-and-breakfast establishments to campsites, shops, restaurants, cafés and public houses – all depend on the trade from tourism, and while the holiday boat-hire business goes to sleep in the winter, many land-based operations look at ways to extend their seasons.

A growing emphasis is being placed on sustainable tourism, where conservation and tourism are mutually beneficial. It is very much a balancing act, but it is in the Broads' best interest to encourage tourism projects which improve the local economy, draw on traditional skills and crafts, and help visitors understand the area's unique character.

Above left: Holiday homes, Horning
Above: Swan Hotel gardens,
River Bure
Below: Traditional Broads sailing
cruisers hauled out for winter refit
at Southgates, Horning

ARTISTIC CONNECTIONS

Of all the influences which the Broads have had on cultural matters, the most memorable can be found in Norwich Castle museum, where many works by the Norwich School of artists are on display. In the late eighteenth and early nineteenth centuries famous painters such as Cotman, Stannard, Crome and Ladbrooke took their inspiration from the Dutch School of Cuyp, Ruisdael and Hobbema, adapting the style to their own surroundings.

It was a fairly easy connection to make. The flat drained marshes of the eastern Broads were similar to Holland, and the region had strong ties there anyway through its proximity across the North Sea, and through the weaving industry. Apart from the Grand Tour collections of Old Masters at Holkham and Felbrigg, countless merchants in Norwich and Great Yarmouth had Dutch paintings hanging on their walls. In fact, it was the collection of a Norwich weaver and merchant, Thomas Harvey, described as 'passionately fond of the arts, and himself no despicable artist', which inspired the young John Crome.

It was a fortunate meeting. Crome, at the start of his painting career, had in Harvey a great patron who not only offered encouragement, but contacts as well. He allowed Crome to copy some of his paintings – by Hobbema and Gainsborough – and introduced the artist to other artists and patrons. In 1803 Crome and Ladbrooke set up the Norwich Society to help foster the works of the growing number of artists in the region. Crome was one of the best interpreters of the English countryside, and although he covered subjects further afield, for many it is his tranquil river views on the Wensum and Yare which rank as his finest work.

With the development of photography in the nineteenth century various people came to the area to interpret the Broads landscapes and industries using the extraordinarily cumbersome equipment of the time. George Christopher Davies is regarded as the first of the Broads photographers. His boundless enthusiasm for this unique landscape manifested itself not just in photographs but in books, his *tour de force* undoubtedly *A Handbook to the Rivers and Broads of Norfolk and Suffolk*, published by Jarrold & Sons of Norwich, which ran to a staggering fifty editions. Whilst Davies' photographs might be considered the works of a gifted amateur, many would consider P.H. Emerson to be the pre-eminent Broads photographer of all time. Born in Cuba in 1856, Emerson had trained as a surgeon before abandoning medicine in favour of photography.

In the late nineteenth century photographers such as Henry Peach Robinson advocated planning out a photograph, even to the point of sketching it out beforehand. Emerson worked on the basis that a scene should be photographed as it was. Even so, he would render the same scene on several different plates to ensure he had captured it the way he wanted, and would experiment with processes such as photogravure and platinum as a means of manipulating the image after exposure. Emerson had argued that photography was art, but that the trouble was that it was imitating the painters of the time. In setting new boundaries for the artform, he ended up not only with many photographers – even to this day – attempting to capture the stylised purity of his photographs, but painters as well.

In the literary field, the Broads area can boast one or two notables. Born in London in 1605, Thomas Browne was a physician and author who travelled

Opposite: Field poppies and wild chamomile, Buckenham

widely in Europe before settling in Norwich in 1637. *Religio Medici* (*The religion of a doctor*), published in 1643, was a justification of his profession, while *Urn Burial* (1658) examined morality and oblivion. Along with his other works, they became accepted as prose masterpieces, and he was knighted in 1671 by Charles II. A statue of Sir Thomas in pensive mood can be found on Hay Hill in Norwich.

Much of the plot of Charles Dickens' *David Copperfield* was set in Great Yarmouth. The author stayed at the Royal Hotel on Marine Parade while he was researching the book. Anna Sewell, author of the children's classic *Black Beauty*, was born in Great Yarmouth in 1820 in a delightful timbered house which still survives, near St Nicholas' church.

While all these can really only be regarded as incidental as far as the Broads are concerned, one famous children's author, Arthur Ransome, featured the Broads in two of his books. Although Ransome's first adventures as a child were on Coniston Water in the Lake District, inspiring his most well-known book, *Swallows and Amazons*, his family were from Norfolk, and Arthur could trace his ancestors back as far as a sixteenth-century Norwich miller. Indeed, one of his forebears was Robert Ransome, a Norwich ironfounder who set up an engineering business in Ipswich in 1789. The business flourished into something of a dynasty, becoming one of the industrial mainstays of Ipswich and East Anglia.

Arthur's first visit to the Broads was in 1919, but it wasn't until 1931 that he returned, and again in 1933, with *Coot Club* coming out the following year. It was a classic children's adventure, followed up with the detective thriller *Big Six*, published in 1940. These sailing adventures undoubtedly helped to promote Broads holidays in a big way. Both books were subsequently serialised for BBC television.

Right: Great Yarmouth quayside and docks

5 Recreation

Well over a million people visit the Broads each year. Around 200,000 of them spend a week or more on a holiday cruiser, so clearly there are many more engaged in a variety of pursuits other than chugging up and down the rivers and mooring up at a staithe or on a river bank each night. As with other National Parks, the policy as far as recreation is concerned is one of promoting 'quiet enjoyment'. This is more critical in the Broads, however, because many of the wildlife habitats are a good deal more sensitive than in the other National Parks, and vulnerable to pressure from inappropriate activities.

It is quite possible for an area to become a victim of its own success, literally to be loved to death. So what is deemed appropriate for one area may not necessarily be fitting for another. Striking that balance can be tricky, but most well-informed people would accept that there are some places where increased numbers of visitors – whether on foot, on wheels, or on the water – would be detrimental to the environment, and others where they would be less so.

FISHING

Back in the days when Victorian holidaymakers were discovering the Broads, the high-quality waters absolutely teemed with fish. The abundance of plantlife in the water provided the habitats in which the fish could flourish. While the subsequent decline in water quality and loss of plantlife has resulted in a decline in the fish stocks, it is all relative. These days, the Rivers Bure, Waveney and Yare, along with their tributaries, and the broads themselves,

Above: Hickling Staithe
Left: Fishing on Filby Broad

Above: Cuckoo *(in black) holding off* Farthing, *in a hard-fought tacking duel on the River Yare, in a manner unchanged in over 100 years*

Opposite: Perched at the end of the bowsprit, a crew member attaches the jib furler. This mechanism remains unchanged since it was introduced by Wykham-Martin, a Victorian gentleman seafarer

still provide some of the finest coarse fishing in the country, with pike, perch, roach, dace and chubb to tempt anglers. Rudd and tench can still be found, but only in those few places where water plants are prolific.

A current Environment Agency licence is required to fish, although many banks on tidal stretches of rivers can be fished for free subject to gaining access. Alternatively, you could hire a boat for the day and fish from that. As with many activities on the Broads, the fact that vehicular access is limited can lead to a conflict of interests. The places with car parking tend also to be river-side moorings, and constant boat traffic and anglers do not mix too well. The over-riding point to remember is that in the summer the main rivers and broads are very busy, so fishing in the early morning and late evening will be far more fruitful (and peaceful). With this in mind the Broads Authority has instituted a zoning arrangement, where boats are requested to keep their distance at various places along the rivers before 9 o'clock on Sunday mornings.

SAILING

Although the Victorians brought an industrial scale to the business of recreation, not just in the Broads but in many seaside resorts and spa towns, people have been having fun here a good deal longer. Water frolics were popular pastimes well before Victoria came to the throne, with both landed gentry and commoners mixing together in a village fête atmosphere. But the nineteenth century saw the development of pleasure sailing boats, and the start of popular and competitive regattas.

The well-heeled would employ skippers to sail the boats, whilst the boat's owner would sit back and enjoy the ride (and, indeed, any glory that was going). Sailing clubs abound in the Broads, and May to September every year sees a full programme of regattas and other events. One of the most exciting,

Above: Rowing near Whittlingham, River Yare

both for competitors and spectators, is the Three Rivers Race at Horning, held over two days in early June every year. All manner of boats take part, sailing up and down the Rivers Ant, Thurne and Bure, the order in which they are tackled dependent on the tides.

Skill was, and still is, a prerequisite for sailing on the Broads. Whilst sea-going yachtsmen may turn up their noses at those sailing the inland waterways, the Broads are characterised by brisk winds and, in many places, limited space for manoeuvring. That demands expertise not required by your average seafarer.

Of all the waterborne pursuits on the Broads, sailing is the most actively encouraged. There are more types of vessel built specifically for sailing on inland waterways here than in any other part of the country. Locally built boats have masts capable of being lowered, and gaff rigs are common, ideal for catching the breezes above the tree tops on a calm day when a conventional rig might be struggling. There are many distinct classes of sailing boat unique to the Broads, including the Brown Boats, or Broads One Designs, originally built with cedar planking, and reputedly almost impossible to capsize. Modern incarnations are made from glass fibre, which provides for a certain amount of amusement, given that the newer Brown Boats are white! Of the various classes built for sailing on the Broads, the one which retains the most of any kind of purist dimension is the Norfolk Dinghy. Clinker built from varnished mahogany, and recognised by a red letter ' B' on their sails, these 14ft (4.25m) long boats are the only Broads class dinghies not to have been reproduced in modern materials.

While there is a small number of sailing craft available for hire, the majority of people sailing on the Broads will use privately owned vessels. The Broads Authority encourages the use of sailing boats over motor boats by operating a differential in the tolls which are charged.

WINDSURFING

The two favourite areas for windsurfing on the Broads are at Hickling and Horsey, and in both cases the sport goes on year round, with windsurfers donning wetsuits to protect against the cold. It is an exhilarating pastime (particularly once you have learned sufficient to be able to stay on the board for more than a few seconds!), and both these sites benefit from the fact that they are large masses of water with unrestricted winds. Having to share the water with other users can be a problem at times; not all motor-boat users are prepared for the speeds which windsurfers can attain, or the sometimes sudden changes of direction. It is also true to say that their ability to manoeuvre in smaller spaces than boats has the potential for windsurfers to go into areas they should avoid, posing consequent risks to the wildlife. As such, windsurfers have a responsibility to ensure that they do not sail into inappropriate areas. Probably the best way to pursue this sport on the Broads would be by joining one of the local windsurfing clubs.

ROWING AND CANOEING

Undoubtedly one of the cheapest ways of getting afloat on the Broads, this is also one of the best ways of getting away from the beaten track. Rowing boats and canoes can negotiate the quieter channels inaccessible to larger craft, and so avoid problems associated with the wash from passing pleasure cruisers on the larger rivers and broads.

There are a number of places on the Broads where Canadian canoes can be hired, either by the day or half day. You are equipped with a personal flotation aid, and given a safety briefing along with some suggestions for where you might like to paddle. So whether you are interested in rowing or paddling for the sake of it, or perhaps as using the rowing boat as a base for fishing or to get a better look at the wildlife with your binoculars, you can be assured that your pursuit is an environmentally friendly one.

PLEASURE CRUISERS

Roughly 5,000 motor boats are registered to use the Broads waterways, around a quarter of which are hire craft, the rest in private ownership. Fortunately they do not all go out at once, although the hire craft are in constant use throughout the summer, so their impact tends to be disproportionate to their numbers. The fact that they are easy to handle makes them popular, and they are equipped as a real 'home from home', with all conveniences – including television sets! But while the larger vessels built for weekly hire are taken up by people looking specifically for a boating holiday on the Broads, there is also a substantial number of smaller day boats available for those who want to take to the water during a visit to the area.

Changeover day for the weekly hire boats is Saturday, so unless you happen to be involved it is sensible not to be too near a boatyard on that day, as they

tend to be busy. In the normal run of things, hirers arrive at intervals through-out the day. They are then taken out on their chosen craft and shown how to handle it. Once the boatyard operator is happy that boat and clients are safe together, they will move their belongings on board and get started on their holiday.

Under way, the secret to an easy life is to use the tides to your advantage. Broads tides flood for about five hours, then ebb for about seven. While there are two high and low tides daily, the times change from day to day at any given place; on average the tides run about an hour later every day. Way up the Broads rivers, near the limits of navigation, the tides are negligible, but at Great Yarmouth the tidal range is well over 6ft (nearly 2m), and can run as fast as 5mph. This is why it is important to get the tides right for a passage through Great Yarmouth in order to go from the northern Broads rivers to the south-ern, and vice versa. Trying to do so when the tide is at full ebb or flood is fraught with danger. Since the tides on all the Broads rivers are controlled by the tidal stream at Yarmouth Bar, it is these times which are the most useful for any boat skipper looking either to moor at Great Yarmouth, or to make passage through Yarmouth. All this should be explained during your briefing when you take possession of the boat.

It's easy to fall into the routine of cruising by day, mooring up at night. Broads cruisers have no navigation lights, and must therefore be moored by nightfall. Moorings can be found in a variety of places; not unexpectedly, the most popular are those which are close to pubs or restaurants. They may charge for the mooring but deduct the cost from the price of any food or drink that is ordered. Many of the boatyards have small marinas which can be used, and there are also the free moorings provided by the Broads Authority at var-ious locations, although these are generally for no more than twenty-four hours. Apart from that, there are plenty of established moorings along the way.

WALKING

While other National Parks have Britain's most popular outdoors leisure pur-suit – walking – as the cornerstone of their recreational remits, the wetland nature of the Broads puts rather less emphasis on this pastime. Indeed, in cer-tain places it is positively discouraged, but for the right reasons. Part of the unique experience of the Broads is the feeling of seclusion from civilisation when you are on the water; it is one of the few places left in the country where you can be on the water with little intrusion from the banks. Inevitably that means walkers will find that not all the waterways are readily accessible from the land. In a lot of places, where there are significant areas of reedswamp along the water margins, it simply wouldn't be practicable.

Even so, there are still plenty of opportunities for walks, be they short walks from car parks, or longer day walks using public transport. Two long-distance footpaths, the Weavers' Way and the Angles Way, pass through the Broads, and in total there are over 185 miles (300km) of definitive footpaths. There is good variety, too, a mixture of open spaces, woodland and waterside paths, well-kept with sturdy stiles and gates, and well waymarked. But notwithstand-ing those boaters who look for the sense of remoteness, a riverside walk in the summer can sometimes leave you wondering whether the boatyards instruct all their clients to wave at anyone on the river banks – in the holiday season, certainly, you could end up with an aching arm!

NOT A GOOD IDEA...

It might seem somewhat perverse to include in a list of recreational pursuits something which is not recommended, but many people are tempted to go swimming in the Broads, particularly on hot sunny days. Despite the major efforts to improve the water qual-ity, the bottom line is that the broads and associated rivers are still lowland waters, and not clean enough for this activity. Should you happen to get any water in your mouth, the risk of Weil's Disease, although comparatively rare, should not be discounted; more certain are the toxic effects of blue-green algae, which forms a scum on the surface of the water in hot weather. In recent summers this has been a big issue with windsurfers on Hickling Broad.

Given the fact that conserva-tion methods encourage the growth of plantlife in the water, the Broads are definitely unsafe for swimming, particularly as there may well be strong currents and tides to contend with as well. As far as boaters are concerned, they should wear a buoyancy aid at all times. If you happen to fall over-board accidentally you could be knocked unconscious, and in any event the coldness of the water and sudden shock of immersion will quite likely hamper your efforts to swim.

Opposite above: Norwich Yacht Station, Riverside Road
Opposite below: Footpath to Salhouse Broad

WHEATFEN – A PRIME FEN-LAND SITE

At Surlingham is Wheatfen, home for many years of the late Ted Ellis, TV naturalist and author. The 130 acres (52.5ha) of marsh carr and woods have been described by another well-known TV naturalist, Professor David Bellamy, as one of the most important sites of its kind: '… in its way,' he said, ' as important as Mount Everest, or the giant redwood forests of America. It is probably the best bit of fen land we have, because we know so much about it.'. There are nearly 2 miles (3km) of footpaths, and a boardwalk to provide wheelchair access.

Above: Phyllis Ellis at Wheatfen
Right: Wheatfen
Opposite: Footpath under Honing Bridge, next to the North Walsham & Dilham Canal

There are many circular walks, details of which are available in Broads Information Centres. Alternatively, you can do a walk which includes the use of public transport. One very pleasant walk runs from Berney Arms railway halt on Halvergate marshes. From here you can wander across the fields to look at the windpump, and then enjoy a pub lunch at the Berney Arms. It is also possible to do a number of walks using the Bittern Line, the railway line which connects Norwich with Sheringham, with stops at the Broads villages of Salhouse, and Hoveton & Wroxham.

WILDLIFE WATCHING

Part of the great joy of the Broads lies in the diversity of wildlife that you are likely to see, whether on land or water. The various nature reserves and wildlife trails help you to appreciate what you are looking at, and to understand why the particular species are here, and not elsewhere.

At Hickling, the largest of the broads, you can take a trip on an electrically powered reed lighter into the heart of the National Nature Reserve, where you may see the rare and beautiful swallowtail butterfly, and marsh harriers. The trip also includes a stop to ascend a tower constructed in the canopy of an oak tree, affording spectacular views of Hickling Broad and the nearby coastline. Another electrically powered reed-lighter trip is available at Ranworth, taking visitors from Ranworth Staithe to the Norfolk Wildlife Trust's Broads Wildlife Centre. Alternatively, you can approach it from the land by following the boardwalk nature trail, which explains how the natural succession from reedbeds to woodland takes place. The Broads Wildlife Centre is an unusual thatched building, floating on pontoons at the edge of Ranworth Inner Broad. Apart from its displays on the Broads and its wildlife, there is also a viewing gallery and binoculars so that visitors can observe the many species of waterfowl on the broad. At How Hill, near Ludham, you can experience the wildlife water trail on board the *Electric Eel*, an Edwardian-style boat which glides silently through the reeds and dykes around the estate. There is also an excellent wildlife walking trail around the nature reserve.

A GOOD DAY OUT

*The Broads area has a great
range of varied tourist attractions.
To name but a few:*

- *The remains of a third-century
  Roman fort can be found at
  Burgh Castle, overlooking the
  River Waveney near Great
  Yarmouth.*
- *In Norwich can be found the
  magnificent Norman cathedral,
  with its graceful flying buttresses
  and the second highest spire in
  the country (after Salisbury in
  Wiltshire), as well as the
  Norman castle keep, which
  overlooks the modern Castle
  Mall shopping centre.*
- *The Bure Valley Railway, a 15in
  narrow gauge railway, runs for 9
  miles (14.5km) from Wroxham,
  in the heart of the Broads, to
  the market town of Aylsham.*
- *The Museum of the Broads, a
  small museum at Stalham, has
  displays of traditional tools, and
  a number of Broads boats.*
- *Somerleyton Hall and Gardens,
  an Anglo-Italian style mansion,
  once the home of Sir Samuel
  Morton Peto, who made his
  fortune out of the railways.*

CYCLING

If cycling to you is all about travelling faster than walking speed, but at a pace leisurely enough to appreciate everything around you, then the Broads is the ideal place. Indeed, what form of land transport could be more appropriate for a National Park than a pollution-free bicycle? Many visitors bring their own bicycles, particularly those visiting in their own boats or camping, but there are many opportunities for hiring. The larger places like Norwich, Great Yarmouth and Lowestoft are all close enough to the Broads to make a day out on a bicycle a practical proposition. And once you get away from the major roads, you'll find a network of quiet minor roads and country lanes, some with just enough of a slope to remind you that Norfolk is not quite the pushover that Noel Coward would have had us believe in *Private Lives*: 'Very flat, Norfolk'.

Everything that makes up the Broads landscape – the tiny villages, churches, pubs, windpumps and waterways – can be explored readily by bicycle. The Broads Authority has produced a number of leaflets detailing Broads Bike Trails, short circular routes up to around 10 miles (16km) which allow plenty of time for exploring places along the way. There are about twelve bicycle hire points located throughout the Broads, providing all-terrain bikes available in a range of sizes, along with helmets and locks at reasonable rates. They can be found in boatyards and riverside shops at all the starting points of the trails, and they will also supply the leaflets detailing the Broads Bike Trails. Most of the centres can also provide tandems, ideal for anyone looking to give someone with, say, a visual or hearing disability a taste of cycling.

CONSERVATION VOLUNTEERS

It may seem a trifle odd to some, but doing voluntary conservation work has become a popular way of spending a break from the normal rigours of life in recent years, and the Broads offers plenty of potential for people who do not

*Pages 86–7: Cycling and horse
riding on Halvergate Marshes
Right: Model garden next to the
Yarmouth line, Strumpshaw*

Above: The Broads Museum, Sutton
Staithe

mind a spot of hard work. Much of the work with volunteers is done in the marshy fen areas, holding the inevitable tide of succession in its tracks. It boils down to 'scrub bashing', clearing alder and willow using saws and power tools, and also keeping the marsh dykes clear. It is not all hard work, though. There will be an opportunity to take a walk or boat ride to look at the wildlife – in fact one of the advantages of working with conservation volunteers is that you get to see parts of the Broads not normally open to the public.

SIGHTSEEING

It might seem like stating the obvious, but many people come to the area to look at the various tourist attractions: mills, museums, stately homes and so on. Within the Broads area, these will be small, and will have some relevance to the area's history or wildlife. Larger attractions will be found outside the Broads, and of course there is plenty to occupy visitors in Norwich and Great Yarmouth.

6 Exploring the Park

ACLE

The town of Acle lies on the main road between Norwich and Yarmouth, with moorings for boats on the Bure about a mile (1.6km) away at Acle Bridge. The old bridge, no longer standing, was the scene of many grisly executions in former times; the hapless criminals were hanged from the parapet and left to rot. No wonder the old bridge had a reputation for being haunted!

BARTON BROAD

Past Ludham and Irstead Shoals, Barton Broad forms part of the channel of its parent river, unlike most broads which are connected to theirs by a dyke. The broad itself, one of the largest of the Norfolk Broads, is owned by the Norfolk Wildlife Trust, and several rare species of bird can be found on the nature reserve. The Broads Authority and partners have carried out a major restoration project at Barton Broad – Clear Water 2000. The project has improved water quality and the landscape of the broad, and is providing new ways for visitors to enjoy the area and learn about its restoration. The solar-powered twelve-seater catamaran *Ra* takes visitors on an environmentally friendly and quiet tour of the broad. It is said that Nelson learned to sail here.

Above: St Michael's, Beccles
Below: Belaugh village

BARTON TURF

A tiny village on the River Ant, just south-west of Stalham, its name harking back to the origins of the Broads and the people who were employed as turf-cutters.

BECCLES

A thriving port back in the days when wherries plied their way up and down the rivers, transporting goods from the sea ports, or from one town to another. Despite modern-day heavy traffic, this old market town is still a good place to visit. The church has a separate tower, 92ft (28m) high, with some superb views out over the surrounding marshes. Its main claim to historical fame is that Nelson's parents were married there.

BELAUGH

An attractive village on the River Bure between Coltishall and Wroxham, overlooked by the church of St Peter at the top of a hill.

BERNEY ARMS

The first safe place for pleasure boats to moor after running the tidal gauntlet of Breydon, and home to one of the least-accessible public houses by land – no roads, only a half-mile walk across the fields from the railway halt. Sharing this isolation is the tallest of the Broads drainage mills. The Berney Arms Mill has been restored to complete working order, and houses an exhibition on windmills.

BRUNDALL

Although very much a dormitory village for Norwich, Brundall is also a busy holiday village on the Yare, the river lined with charming cottages and villas. Many of the Broads boat-hire companies are based here.

BURGH CASTLE

In Roman times, the waterways of Broadland were far more extensive than they are today; what is now flat marshland was then under the sea. The fort of *Gariannonum* was built on the banks of the vast estuary, with the town of Caister on the opposite bank. Now all that remains of this huge river is Breydon Water, the ruins of the castle standing at the southern end, at the confluence of the rivers Waveney and Yare.

BURGH ST PETER

Travellers on the Waveney cannot fail to notice the striking church out in the marshes on a bend in the river, looking like a pile of children's building blocks placed one on top of the other. Overlooking Oulton Broad, the church, with its sixteenth-century tower, has an even older thatched nave, which is unusually narrow.

Below: Breydon Water

BUNGAY

A prosperous town in times past, the rather odd name is probably derived from 'bongue', a good ford, or 'le bon eye', a spit of land thrusting out into a river. Trading wherries used to sail through Geldeston Lock near Beccles (now the limit of navigation), up the Waveney as far as Bungay. Certainly it was an important crossing point for the Romans – Stane Street ran right through here to *Venta Icenorum*, the Roman town just south of present-day Norwich.

COCKSHOOT BROAD

Near Woodbastwick, this is one of the Broads Authority's first great successes, and a demonstration that nature has the power to recover once the conditions are right. The broad, once mud-filled and lifeless, is now clear and teeming with wildlife and plants. A boarded walkway leads to a bird hide for public use overlooking the broad.

COLTISHALL

Head of navigation on the River Bure, Coltishall is popular with anglers, and also well-known for its nearby RAF station. Made famous during the Battle of Britain by the presence of Douglas Bader, the base was for many years the home of the Battle of Britain Flight of Spitfires, Hurricanes and a Lancaster, before it relocated to RAF Coningsby in Lincolnshire.

Above: Cockshoot Dyke
Below: Coltishall Staithe, River Bure

GREAT YARMOUTH

Popular east-coast seaside resort, with the seafront lined with funfairs and amusement arcades. But Yarmouth has a long and fascinating history as the world's capital of herring fishing, and while much of the town's interesting architecture was lost to World War II bombing and subsequent unsympathetic redevelopment, there is still plenty of interest. Parts of the town's 7ft (2m) thick medieval walls survive, including several of the sixteen towers that punctuated its length. One of them, the North-West Tower on North Quay, is now a Broads Authority Information Centre.

HADDISCOE

This is the village which gave its name to the new cut between Reedham and St Olaves. Built in 1832, the idea, ill-fated as it was, was to provide a short cut for coastal vessels heading for Norwich without their having to pass Great Yarmouth and thus incur tolls. The village itself has a church dating back to the eleventh century, with a floor stone commemorating 'Bele', the wife of one of the Dutchmen responsible for the drainage of the surrounding marshes.

HALVERGATE MARSHES

One of the jewels in the crown of Broadland, Halvergate represents the largest single piece of the uniquely beautiful grazing marshland in the country. With cows grazing on lush green fields criss-crossed with drainage dykes, and windpumps dotted about, the landscape has a serene character which inspired members of the famous Norwich School of painters.

Above: The North West Tower of Great Yarmouth town wall, AD 1344, now houses a Broads Authority information centre and wherry exhibition
Left: Horsing around, Halvergate Marshes

Above: Mississippi showboat, Horning
Below: How Hill gardens and the River Ant
Opposite: Private water garden, How Hill estate

HICKLING

The broad and much of the surrounding area forms a National Nature Reserve managed jointly by English Nature and the Norfolk Wildlife Trust. Boats are allowed only along the marked channels. There are walking trails and a visitor centre, but the best way to see the reserve is by taking the water trail, a 2½ hour guided tour arranged by the Norfolk Wildlife Trust. Up to twelve visitors at a time are taken by boat to see a variety of the features of the broads: reed and sedge beds, marshes and woodlands, and birds, such as the marsh harrier, can be seen from the hides.

HORNING

While Horning has become quite a boating centre, it is not as commercialised as Wroxham, and its charming main street of thatched houses runs parallel to the River Bure for about a mile (1.6km). There are plenty of moorings at the various public houses and hotels along the river; one particularly historic public house is at Horning Ferry. This point has witnessed various means of crossing from one bank to the other for the last 1,000 years. Certainly the old chain ferry, which no longer exists, operated here for many years.

HORSEY

Horsey Mere is about a mile (1.6km) up Meadow Dyke from Heigham Sound, and at the eastern end stands Horsey windpump. Owned by the National Trust, this most impressive landmark affords some fine views across the marshes. The sea is very close here, within a couple of miles.

HOW HILL

This impressive thatched house with pargetting around the windows isn't as old as it looks, built in 1904. The house and grounds were used by Norfolk Education Committee for residential field studies courses up until 1983. Now the 365-acre (148ha) estate is run by the How Hill Trust and the Broads Authority as an environmental education centre and nature reserve.

There are three windpumps on the estate, including Boardman's Mill, a fascinating open-framed timber trestle windpump. Downstream from Boardman's Mill, on the opposite bank of the Ant, is Turf Fen windpump. It is a tower windpump with a double scoop wheel. Also in the grounds, and well worth a look, is Toad Hole Cottage, a marsh-man's cottage. Once the home of an eel-catcher, it has been restored to give a wonderful feel for Victorian country living. The reserve has a walking trail, and visitors can take a ride in the *Electric Eel*, a quiet, electrically powered boat, along a water trail.

Above: The wherry Hathor *on Lake Lothing, Lowestoft*
Below: Ludham village

LODDON

The Chet winds through wooded countryside and marshes, the bridge at the boundary between Loddon and Chedgrave being its navigable head. Once a port for the wherries carrying their cargoes from one Broads town to another, Loddon is a pretty market town which has retained its ancient atmosphere.

LOWESTOFT

The most easterly town in Britain, this fishing port is also a popular holiday town. Only a stone's throw from the Broads, and at the northern tip of the Suffolk Heritage Coast, it is a good base for exploration. The beaches are sandy and safe for bathing, with the north beach at Corton designated a naturists' beach. The harbour is a bustling place, full of interest.

LUDHAM

An attractive village with a large fourteenth-century church dedicated to St Catherine. Although not open for casual visitors, the *Albion*, the most famous of the broad's trading wherries, is based at nearby Womack Water.

MARTHAM

Martham's Georgian houses and cottages are attractively grouped around The Green. The broad itself is actually closer to the head of the river at West Somerton. Access for boats to the largest of the Broads, Hickling Broad, and Horsey Mere, is up Candle Dyke, roughly halfway along the Thurne between Potter Heigham and Martham. Past Heigham Sound the channel divides into two, Hickling Broad at the head of one, and Horsey Mere up the other.

NORWICH

Norfolk's county town and cathedral city, situated on the River Wensum. Although the castle and cathedral date back to Norman times, the city itself is older, based on an Anglo-Saxon settlement. The early Norman castle was in fact a wooden fort, replaced in the twelfth century by a stone keep. For much its history, the castle has been the county gaol of Norfolk, but in the last century, it has been home to an important museum of local history and art. It holds an unrivalled collection of paintings from the famous Norwich School of artists, including those by Crome, Cotman, Ladbroke and Stannard, who took their inspiration from the Dutch School of Cuyp, Ruisdael and Hobbema, and adapted the style to their own surroundings.

What was once the Old Cattle Market, latterly an unsightly car park, has been transformed in recent years into the Castle Mall. Much of the development is in fact underground, with several floors of the shopping mall and car park below ground level, grassed over on top to form a small park which extends to the gardens around the castle itself. Because of the close proximity of the site to the castle, an extensive archaeological dig took place before the development started, revealing a good deal about the Anglo-Saxon settlement which preceded the Norman one.

The cathedral, started in 1096 by Bishop Herbert de Losinga, was built using stone from Normandy, brought upriver to Pull's Ferry, and then along a specially dug canal to the site. Despite being virtually finished twenty-five years later, when de Losinga died, the cathedral was not actually consecrated until 1278. Since then, this magnificent building has been subjected to fires, riots and extensive damage caused by natural phenomena. During World War II it was a target for Hitler's Baedeker raids.

Above: Norwich castle
Pages 98–9: Norwich cathedral

The cathedral close holds an attractive collection of medieval houses and buildings, including the King Edward VI school, whose most famous pupil, without doubt, was Horatio Nelson. In a quiet spot near the cathedral is the grave of nurse Edith Cavell, shot by the Germans in 1915 for helping allied prisoners to escape. Her memory is also perpetuated by a statue outside the close in Tombland. Nearby is the Maid's Head Hotel, thought by some to be the oldest inn in the country, and the starting-off point for the first regular stagecoach service between Norwich and London.

About 2 miles (3.2km) from the city centre, in the grounds of the University of East Anglia, stands the Sainsbury Centre. This is Norman Foster's award-winning space-age building housing Robert and Lisa Sainsbury's famous art collection, along with regular displays of national exhibitions.

OULTON BROAD

Connected to the Waveney by Oulton Dyke, the broad can sometimes look like an overgrown boating pond. Next door to the seaside resort of Lowestoft, Oulton Broad attracts vast numbers of sailing vessels and motor boats, and is also the scene of powerboat racing. Like its neighbour, it has suffered at the hands of commercialisation.

POSTWICK

A village situated in a loop of the River Yare just outside Norwich. Parts of All Saints Church date back to the thirteenth century.

POTTER HEIGHAM

With a headroom of only 7ft (2m), the old bridge at Potter Heigham has been the downfall of many a holiday sailor. In other words, if in doubt, it's best to wait for low tide! One mile (1.6km) north lies the village itself which, as the name suggests, was the site of a Roman pottery. The church is interesting, with its thatched nave, and typical Norfolk round tower supporting an octagonal belfry.

RANWORTH

No trip to the Broads, whether by land or water, should omit a visit to Ranworth. The view from the tower of St Helen's Church is magnificent. The church also has one of the finest and best preserved painted rood screens in the country. The Broads Wildlife Centre can be reached by following the nature trail through the woods and marshes to the unique thatched building, floating on pontoons at the edge of Ranworth Broad. The building houses an excellent display illustrating the diversity of interests in the Broads, and you can also sit in the upper gallery overlooking the broad (closed to boats) and observe many different species of waterfowl through the binoculars and telescopes provided.

Opposite: View from Ranworth church tower
Below: Reedham chain ferry

REEDHAM

Provides the only crossing over the Yare between Norwich and Yarmouth. Driven by a diesel engine, the chain ferry clanks across the river. Reedham is traditionally the seat of the East Anglian martyr King Edmund, killed by the Danes in AD870 for refusing to renounce Christianity.

ROCKLAND ST MARY

Rockland Broad is the largest broad off the River Yare, supporting water-lilies and the rare compressed river mussel. The village became the first parish in the country to claim ownership of its own broad, which it did in 2000.

ST BENET'S ABBEY

The ruin of St Benet's Abbey is unmistakable, with a windmill built into the remaining walls of the gatehouse some 200 years ago. The first abbey was destroyed by the Danes in AD870, and was later rebuilt by King Canute. When the Normans invaded, the Benedictine monastery held out in a state of siege for four months, until it fell to them through the treachery of one of the lay brothers. When it was all over, the Normans made him Abbot of St Benet's for life, and then promptly strung him up on a gibbet as a reward for his treachery.

ST OLAVES

A popular place for mooring, St Olaves has the remains of a thirteenth-century priory, notable for its undercroft, a very early brick construction.

SALHOUSE

To the east of Wroxham, just past Wroxham Broad, is Salhouse Broad, and the village of Salhouse, about a half a mile away along a pleasant footpath. The twelfth-century church of All Saints has a somewhat curious lop-sided appearance, the legacy of unfinished subsequent work.

SOMERLEYTON

The River Waveney passes close by this attractive Victorian estate village, with red-brick cottages grouped around the green. Somerleyton Hall dates back to Elizabethan times, although extensively rebuilt in 1846 by Sir Samuel Morton Peto, who had made his fortune building railways. The mansion has some lavishly furnished state rooms, and the gardens include a maze.

SOUTH WALSHAM

South Walsham Inner Broad is private, and although sailing is permitted, fishing, swimming and mooring are not. By road, South Walsham is a stone's throw from Ranworth, and the church of St Mary contains a fifteenth-century rood screen. St Lawrence's Church, in the same churchyard, fell into disrepair after it was damaged by fire some 160 years ago.

STALHAM

A pleasant little market town, ideally situated for exploring Barton and Hickling Broads, and quite close to the seaside towns of Happisburgh and Sea Palling. Stalham is also a good starting point for walking the Weaver's Way footpath.

Above: A German pleasure boat, unclaimed at the end of World War II, in Salhouse Broad
Opposite: Thatched cottage, South Walsham

STOKESBY

Isolated and utterly charming, Stokesby is a pretty riverside red-brick village, with thatched church nearby. It is the first village along the River Bure from Yarmouth towards Acle, with plenty of moorings at the Ferry Inn for anyone looking for a little light refreshment.

SURLINGHAM

Surlingham Broad is the biggest of a group of small broads linked together by a series of waterways. The lesser broads are not open to navigation, and the whole swamp-like area forms a nature reserve owned by the Norfolk Wildlife Trust. Nearby Surlingham Church Marsh (RSPB) is a former grazing marsh, home to ringed plovers and terns. A circular walk of about 1½ miles (2.4km) can be taken around the marsh, starting from the church. Also at Surlingham is Wheatfen, home for many years of the late Ted Ellis, TV naturalist and author. The 130 acres (52.5ha) of marsh carr and woods have been described by Professor David Bellamy as one of the most important sites of its kind.

SUTTON

At the head of Sutton Broad, to the east of the River Ant, lies the village of Sutton. Just east of the village on the road to Hickling stands Sutton Mill, at 75ft (23m) the tallest surviving tower windmill in the country. It was built in 1789, with nine floors, and was last used in the 1940s. An adjacent building houses an extensive museum.

THORPE ST ANDREW

The smart residential suburb of Thorpe St Andrew is just east of Norwich on the Yare. Thorpe village itself is on the delightful backwater of the Old River. In 1844 a new cut was dug from one corner of the loop in the river to the other, improving the passage of commercial ships heading for Norwich, which previously had to negotiate two railway bridges. Across the river, with access from Trowse, is Whitlingham Country Park.

THURNE

Just north of the point where the River Thurne joins the Bure is the unspoilt village of Thurne. At the entrance to Thurne Dyke is a pretty windpump with a white-painted tower, undoubtedly one of the most distinctive of all the Broadland windpumps. Just downriver is the other windpump at Thurne, the St Benet's Level windpump.

UPTON

Just north of Acle, Upton features a number of houses scattered around the green, while a gravestone with a carving of a wherry in the nearby churchyard reminds us of the connections with the traditional broads cargo carrier.

WOODBASTWICK

A pretty estate village of thatched cottages grouped around a green. Dating from the fourteenth century, the church is dedicated to St Fabian and St Sebastian, unique in this country. North-east of Woodbastwick, starting

Right: St Fabian & St Sebastian, Woodbastwick

from the end of Ferry Road, is the boardwalk nature trail which leads to Cockshoot Broad.

WORSTEAD

The village of Worstead gave its name to the cloth it produced, which first gained popularity in the thirteenth century. When Edward III married Philippa of Hainault, the import of foreign material was banned, giving the home weaving industry a valuable fillip. As a result, Flemish weavers came over to this country, settling in East Anglia, and bringing their style of architecture and culture with them. Many of their old houses can still be seen in Worstead.

WROXHAM

If Wroxham is regarded as the capital of the Broads, then the Bure could be called its high street. Many boating holidays start from here, and the banks of the river are lined with boatyards crowded with Broads cruisers. It was here that the concept of boating holidays started just over a century ago. Since then, the twin villages of Wroxham and Hoveton St John have grown into a thriving tourist centre.

Above: Congested traffic at Wroxham, River Bure
Opposite: Footpath along the North Walsham & Dilham Canal

Information

USEFUL ADDRESSES

Broads Authority
Thomas Harvey House
18 Colegate
Norwich NR3 1BQ
Tel: 01603 610734
Email: broads@broads-
authority.gov.uk
www.broads-authority.gov.uk

Broads Society
6 Marie Close
Cantley
Norwich NR13 3RN
Tel: 01493 700344
www.broads-society.org.uk

East of England Tourist Board
Toppesfield Hall
Hadleigh
Suffolk IP7 5DN
Tel: 01473 822922
Web:
www.eastofenglandtouristboard.com

English Heritage
23 Savile Row
London W1X 1AB
Tel: 0207 973 3250
www.english-heritage.org.uk

English Nature
60 Bracondale
Norwich NR1 2BE
Tel: 01603 620558
Web: www.english-nature.org.uk

Environment Agency
Anglian Region Office
Kingfisher House
Goldhay Way
Orton Goldhay
Peterborough PE2 5ZR
Tel: 01733 371811
www.environment-agency.gov.uk

Great Yarmouth Port Authority
20 South Quay
Great Yarmouth
Tel: 01493 335500

National Trust
East Anglian Regional Office
Blickling
Norwich NR11 GNF
Tel: 01263 733471
www.nationaltrust.org.uk

Norfolk Ornithologists
    Association
Aslack Way
Holme-next-the-Sea
near Hunstanton
Tel: 01485 25266

Norfolk Wildlife Trust
72 Cathedral Close
Norwich NR1 4DF
Tel: 01603 625540
www.wildlifetrust.org.uk/norfolk

Norfolk Windmills Trust
Tel: 01603 222705

Royal Society for the Protection
    of Birds
97 Yarmouth Road
Norwich NR7 0HF
Tel: 01603 700880
www.rspb.org.uk

Suffolk Wildlife Trust
Brooke House
The Green
Ashbocking
Ipswich IP6 9JY
Tel: 01473 890089
www.wildlifetrust.org.uk/suffolk

Suffolk Windmills Trust
Tel: 01473 890089

Wildfowl and Wetlands Trust
Slimbridge
Gloucestershire GL2 7BT
Tel: 01453 89333
www.wwt.org.uk

BROADS INFORMATION CENTRES

Beccles
The Quay
Fen Lane
Tel: 01502 713196

Great Yarmouth
North-West Tower
North Quay
Tel: 01493 332095

Hoveton
Station Road
Tel: 01603 782281

Loddon
The Old Town Hall
1 Bridge Street
Tel: 01508 521028

Potter Heigham
The Staithe
Tel: 01692 670779

Ranworth
The Staithe
Tel: 01603 270453

Toad Hole Cottage
How Hill
Ludham
Tel: 01692 678763

Winter enquiries:
Broads Authority, as above

TOURIST INFORMATION CENTRES

Aylsham
Bure Valley Railway Station
Norwich Road
Tel: 01263 733903

Great Yarmouth
Town Hall
Hall Quay
Tel: 01493 846345
Marine Parade
Tel: 01493 842195
Email: tourism@great-yarmouth.gov.uk
www.great-yarmouth.gov.uk

Lowestoft
The East Point Pavilion
Tel: 01502 533600
Email:
touristinfo@waveney.gov.uk
www.visit_lowestoft.co.uk

Norwich
The Guildhall
Gaol Hill
Tel: 01603 666071
Email:
tourism.norwich@gtnet.gov.uk
www.norwich.gov.uk

PLACES TO VISIT

Berney Arms Mill
near Reedham
Tel: 01604 730320

Broads Wildlife Centre
Ranworth
Tel: 01603 270479

Burgh Castle
near Great Yarmouth

Fairhaven Garden Trust
South Walsham
Tel: 01603 270449
www.Fairhavengroup.co.uk/
garden-trust.htm

Hickling Broad
Hickling
Tel: 01692 598276

How Hill
near Ludham
Tel: 01692 678763

Horsey Windpump
Horsey
near Winterton
Tel: 01493 393904

Museum of the Broads
The Staithe
Stalham NR12 9DA
Tel: 01692 581681

Web: www.whiteswan.u-net.com
Pettits of Reedham
Camp Hill, Reedham

Somerleyton Hall
Somerleyton
near Lowestoft
Tel: 01502 730224
www.somerleyton.co.uk

St Benet's Abbey
near Ludham

St Olaves Priory
near Beccles

Stracey Arms Windpump
near Acle
Tel: 01603 222705

Thurne Dyke Windpump
Thurne

MAPS

A good quality map enables you to gain a much better appreciation of the countryside:
OS Outdoor Leisure Map 40 The Broads (1:25,000), available in standard and waterproof editions
OS Landranger 134 Norwich and the Broads (1:50,000)
GEOprojects The Broads, available in standard and waterproof editions

FURTHER READING

Bowskill, Derek. *The Norfolk Broads & Fens: A cruising guide to the waterways of East of England* (Opus Book Publishing, 1999)

Campbell, Jamie & Middleton, Cliff. *The man who found the Broads: A biography of George Christopher Davies* (Hamilton Publications, 1999)

Denyer, Richard. *Still Waters* (The Norfolk Broads Yacht Company, 1989)

Denyer, Richard. *Wetlands* (Sidgwick & Jackson, 1990)

Edwards, Rod. *A Breath of East Anglia* (Jarrolds Publishing, 1999)

Ewans, Martin. *The Battle for the Broads* (Terence Dalton, 1992)

George, Martin. *Land use, ecology and conservation of Broadland* (Packard Publishing, 1992)

Hamilton's Navigations (Hamilton Publications, 1997)

Hedley, Miles. *Still Waters: a portrait of Broadland today* (Maas Books, 1999)

Holmes, David. *Back to the Broads* (Sutton Publishing, 1998)

Holmes, David. *The Norfolk Broads in old photographs* (Sutton Publishing, 1996)

Lambert, Dr Joyce, Jennings, J.N., Smith, C.T., Green, Charles, and Hutchinson, J.N. *The Making of the Broads* (Royal Geographical Society/John Murray, 1960)

Malster, Robert. *The Broads* (Phillimore, 1993)

What to do on the Norfolk Broads (Jarrold Publishing, annual)

Williamson, Tom. *The Norfolk Broads: A Landscape History* (Manchester University Press, 1997)

OTHER REFERENCE

www.norfolkbroads.com

www.nbyco.com
This website is maintained by The Norfolk Broads Yachting Company as an information point for visitors and those from outside the area – it contains over 200 photographs from Victorian times up to the present day, with captions and explanations of interest to anyone seeking more information on the Broads.

Below: Pier and fishing boats at Cromer on the north Norfolk coast

Index

Page numbers in *italics* indicate illustrations